Chaim Walder

People Speak 5

Stories that speak to you...

Translated by Chani Goldwasser

FELDHEIM PUBLISHERS
JERUSALEM   NEW YORK

Originally published in Hebrew as
Anashim Mesaprim al Atzmam 5

ISBN 978-1-59826-898-0

Copyright © 2012 by Chaim Walder

All rights reserved.
No part of this publication may be translated,
reproduced, stored in a retrieval system or transmitted,
in any form or by any means, electronic, mechanical,
photocopying, recording or otherwise, even for personal use,
without written permission from the publisher.

Edited and typeset by Eden Chachamtzedek

FELDHEIM PUBLISHERS
POB 43163 / Jerusalem, Israel

10 9 8 7 6 5 4 3 2 1

Printed in Israel

To my first grandson, Itamar, *n"y*
And to his parents, Tzviki and Yaffi, *n"y*
Beloved and significant chapters
In the story of my life

Contents

1: The Red Handkerchief 9
2: The Will 16
3: Who Is a Champion 28
4: Nursing Home 39
5: The Fateful *Farher* 48
6: The Bodyguard 57
7: Kindness over Cruelty 70
8: The Chef 85
9: A Simple Jew 97
10: The Dirty Side of Cleanliness 104
11: Seeking Atonement 111
12: A Letter to Daddy and Mommy 121
13: A Stab to the Heart 126
14: Covered for Life 137
15: The Reward for Humiliation 144
16: Peace at Home 150
17: A Costly *Simchah* 159

18: Pictures of Life *169*
19: The Reward for a *Kabbalah* *179*
20: Building Number Eighteen *188*
21: The Power of Prayer *198*
22: The Only Thing to Fear Is Fear Itself *205*
23: Deceptive Garbage *211*
24: The Grand Scheme *224*

Glossary *235*

The Red Handkerchief

Is there anything more annoying than a traffic cop lying in wait at an intersection in order to slap drivers with a ticket?

A goodhearted citizen whose building was being used by the police for this purpose decided to put an end to the matter! He acted with determination and even took on the police department in court.

He really did put an end to the matter, but not the end he planned...

Despite the important lesson inherent in this story, I've waited with it for twenty years. The reason for the delay will soon become clear.

I live in a building located at a very busy intersection that has no traffic light. Near our building is a stop sign, and when you turn right, there's a crosswalk.

For some reason, probably ideal topographical conditions, traffic cops often wait a few yards after the crosswalk, where they pull over drivers who failed to stop at the intersection or who failed to yield the right of way to pedestrians at the crosswalk. The law is that at a crosswalk, drivers are obligated to stop for pedestrians who have stepped off the curb into the street, but the fact is that many drivers ignore this law.

Over the years, thousands of drivers have been slapped with tickets right under our building, and this goes on to this day. How come? Because people who don't obey traffic laws will be caught again and again — if not at our intersection, then at another.

They usually blame their bad luck, but if they were to consider the situation, they would realize that when a person almost never stops at a stop sign and almost always fails to allow pedestrians the right of way at a crosswalk, it's only a matter of time until a policeman waiting at an intersection somewhere catches him on some violation. Their luck is no worse than anyone else's, but someone who obeys the law doesn't *need* luck. He doesn't get caught simply because he does nothing wrong.

As one who observes the ticket-giving process up close, I can tell you that sometimes it seems that police officers get actual pleasure out of writing out those tickets. What really gets me is when they give a ticket to a driver who actually stopped at the stop sign, but just rolled a tiny drop over the crosswalk line. Sometimes it seems as if these officers don't really care whether or not the driver they're ticketing has behaved irresponsibly — all they seem to care about is fulfilling their quota of tickets.

I don't mean to make light of traffic laws, but I think that the *point* of the law should be taken into account, not just the picayune details.

The residents of our building took pity on drivers who were stopped and ticketed. We used to watch with interest the drastic differences in the way the various drivers responded

The Red Handkerchief

to the situation. Some pretended they couldn't care less, accepting the ticket, thanking the police officer, and driving on, while others wept, wailed and pleaded — or alternatively, cursed and threatened the police officer.

Not that this has anything to do with my story, but I have reached the conclusion that neither approach has an advantage over the other. From my observation post, I saw that the deciding factor in whether a driver will or won't get a ticket is whether or not the police officer takes a liking to him. Sometimes the officer softens upon hearing a personal story, whereas other times, it only make him harsher. "Your child is sick? Is that any reason to endanger his life?" As with everything in life, praying to "find favor in the eyes of God and man" is the best bet.

Back to the story.

One day, my upstairs neighbor decided to do something about the situation. Every time he saw a police car parked under our building, he'd tape a big piece of paper to the bottom of the stop sign, with the words: "Warning! Traffic cop parked just around the corner," in large letters.

He explained that he felt bad that so many drivers had to pay fines. "Besides," he added, "I want the police to leave our area and choose a different spot. I don't like it that so many people get upset and curse near our building."

Do you think the police left?

No way. They found out what had been going on, and although it isn't clear who ratted on the neighbor, they paid him a visit and warned him to stop.

"Okay," he replied. So for the next week, he abstained from hanging up the sign, but after that, he went back to his old ways, hanging up the sign whenever he saw the police cruiser near our building.

The next time, they arrested him on charges of "interfering with a law enforcement officer in the line of duty," and he was given a trial date. In the meantime, he continued hanging the sign.

We tried to persuade him to stop, as it would only get him into more trouble, but there was no swaying him. He'd made up his mind to go all the way.

At a certain point, he had to pay a fine. He paid it and continued hanging the sign.

The police officers took the matter personally, perhaps because there was a considerable reduction in the number of tickets issued. It's not as if they were left with nothing to do; there were still plenty of drivers who broke the law. Maybe they didn't see the sign, or maybe they were too engrossed in an interesting conversation to check what it said.

When he was arrested for the second time, our neighbor was brought before a judge who warned him that if he hung the sign again, he'd go to jail. That finally convinced him to stop, because he wasn't prepared to be locked up over someone else's traffic violations.

A few days passed and the tickets were being issued thick and fast again, when our neighbor came up with a new idea.

He purchased a huge red handkerchief. For the next week, he stood at the intersection and told drivers that from now on, the red handkerchief would be replacing the sign. Every time there was a red handkerchief flapping in the wind from the roof of our building, it meant that the police were waiting around the corner.

Once again, the volume of tickets began decreasing significantly.

The Red Handkerchief

The police officers were no fools, and they soon figured out the connection between the red handkerchief and the reduction in tickets. They returned and arrested our neighbor once again.

Once again, the man was brought before the judge. A number of neighbors, myself included, accompanied him to the courthouse, to offer support should he receive a jail sentence. I intended to plead with the judge to go easy on him, though I wasn't sure what reasons I'd give. The truth is that I was really just curious to see what would happen.

It turned out that my neighbor didn't need my speech. He managed just fine on his own.

When he was put on the stand, the prosecutor asked him, "Do you understand that you are being charged with interfering with police officers' work."

"How exactly am I interfering?" he responded.

"By warning drivers of police presence at the intersection."

"That's a lie. I'm afraid of *ayin hara*, that's all. That's why I hang a red handkerchief from my roof. How can you prevent me from doing that?"

Everyone chuckled, including the judge.

The debate began. The prosecutor argued that the man was making a laughingstock of the court, but the judge ruled that even if it presented a problem, there really was no law forbidding a citizen from hanging a rag of the color of his choice from the roof of the building he lived in. To the dismay of the police representatives and their lawyers, he acquitted the man, not before adding, "I don't understand what you have against the police. All they're trying to do is prevent traffic violations. You're very clever, but you're not right."

"Well, then," replied my neighbor, "I'm just fulfilling the well-known saying: 'On the road, don't be right; be smart!'

Everyone laughed — even the police representatives and their lawyers.

A month passed and the joke became the saddest thing you'd ever heard.

It happened in the afternoon. There was an accident at the intersection. A car hit a thirty-five-year-old pedestrian.

It was immediately obvious that this was a very serious accident. The man was flung into the air by a speeding car and hurled against a pole.

He was still breathing when they whisked him off to the hospital, but tragically he never regained consciousness. Mourning announcements were plastered all over our building.

Why our building? Because the accident victim was the son of our upstairs neighbor, the one who had warned drivers about the traffic cop parked around the corner.

At the police interrogation, the driver was asked why he had been driving so carelessly and why he hadn't stopped at the stop sign.

"Because there was no handkerchief," he replied, without batting an eyelash.

"There was no *what?*' the investigators asked.

He told them that every time he passed by that intersection, he would glance upward. If he saw a red handkerchief waving from the roof of the building on the corner, he was careful to heed the law. If not, he would speed by, safe in the knowledge that there was no police presence.

In this case, there weren't any officers, but there was someone else at the crosswalk... the son of the man who used to hang the handkerchief.

The Red Handkerchief

That's the story. It happened twenty years ago, and I'm sure the lesson it teaches speaks for itself.

Before now, no one spoke openly about what had happened because we didn't want to add to our neighbor's heartache — and believe me, he'd had more than enough of that. No one told him a word, but guilt waved like a red handkerchief in front of his eyes. His chuckle at the courthouse was the last time I ever heard him laugh. He lived out the rest of his years filled with anguished regret.

We all attended his *levayah,* yet not a single one of us voiced what he was thinking in his heart.

He was buried near his son.

It was a tragic *levayah,* because everyone knew the terrible story behind his son's death.

At the end of the *levayah,* the widow rose and faced the old grave and the fresh one.

"God in Heaven knows that you meant well," she said. "He knows how much you suffered. He knows that while you were buried today, your heart died twenty years ago. You asked Him for forgiveness every night, but you never knew peace. Only death could bring you that. Now you're finally reunited with our precious son. God knows that you've received your punishment in this world."

And then she withdrew the red handkerchief and lay it gently on top of both the old grave and the fresh one.

The Will

The hero of this story, our favorite Yerushalmi, returns with a story that begins more than seventy years ago and will never come to an end...

This time, we meet his childhood friend, Leibele, whose ninety some odd years did nothing to erase his inner mischievousness.

Leibele asked the contributor of this story to sign his "second will."

The obvious question is: What was his first will?

The answer is one of the funniest, most surprising and touching story you've ever heard.

Dear Mr. Chaim Walder,
This is the Yerushalmi *Yid* who writes to you *every* now and again.

I was very surprised to see that you included four of my letters in your last book, plus the big surprise you prepared for me at the end: a letter from my wife, may she be well. It wasn't really a surprise, because she'd let slip a few times that she was planning to write to you, though I always pretended not to have heard. I even hurried to warn you that

The Will

you might receive a letter from her. Still, it *was* a surprise because I didn't know the contents of the letter until I read it in your book.

Now I'd like to tell you about my friend Leibele, whom I've never mentioned before.

The story took place many years ago, when I ran into Leibele in shul one day.

To be perfectly honest, my meeting Leibele was no big deal, as I'd been meeting him pretty much every day for the past eighty years — ever since we attended *cheder* together in Meah Shearim, and later on, in yeshivah and in shul after we both married. Neither of us ever left Eretz Yisrael; in fact, we very rarely left our neighborhood.

In his youth, Leibel was a big troublemaker, but he had a heart of gold. I personally owe him a debt of gratitude for rescuing me from one of the principals of the Talmud Torah of whom I was terrified — with good reason.

My *melamed* at the time seemed to have something against me and he would often give me a slap and send me to the *menahel* over the littlest thing.

One time, as I was on my way down the hall to the *menahel*'s office for a punishment, Leibele came hurrying down the hall after me. "Wait a minute," he said. "I'll go to the *menahel* instead of you." Before I could object, he'd taken off in the direction of the *menahel*'s office. Ten minutes later, he brought me a note signed by the *menahel*. It bore a few words of reprimand and expressed the hope that I would refrain from talking during class in the future. He stuck the note into my hand, saying, "The *menahel* forgives you." I brought the note to my *melamed*, who glanced at it and told me to take my seat — but not before adding a few more reprimands.

From that point on, whenever I was sent to the *menahel*, Leibele would follow me, stop me in the hallway, leave for a few moments and return with a note from the *menahel*.

This arrangement might have gone on forever, or at least until I completed my studies at the Talmud Torah, but one day, after a lesson during which I'd been sent out of class and had later returned with the help of a note from the *menahel* procured by Leibele, the *menahel* and the *melamed* suddenly appeared in the doorway of my classroom and summoned me over.

The *melamed* showed me the note and asked, "Who wrote this?"

"The *menahel*," I replied.

"Were you in my office?" the *menahel* asked.

"No, but Leibele went in my place, and he brought me the note."

Well, you can probably imagine what happened after that. Leibele was summoned to the hallway, where he was forced to admit that he'd never actually visited the *menahel*'s office. All those times he'd brought me a note "from the *menahel*," he had, in fact, simply entered an empty classroom and written the note himself. It looked so much like one of the *menahel*'s notes — flowery signature and all — that even the *menahel* himself had a hard time figuring out that it was a forgery.

Of course, Leibele received a punishment that was far greater than all the punishments that he'd spared me from, and we were both sent home from *cheder*.

"Why'd you do it?" I asked him on our way home.

"I saw you suffering, and I couldn't take it anymore. I wouldn't have done it for a troublemaker, but you, *nebach*

The Will

— you don't do anything wrong! The *melamed* picks on you for no reason! I couldn't sit by and let that happen."

"I understand," I told him. "But how were you able to do a thing like that? How you were able to forge the *menahel*'s handwriting?"

"Oh, that?" Leibele shrugged. "No problem. I have lots of notes from the *menahel* at home. I studied his handwriting until I could copy it perfectly."

It didn't occur to Leibele that my question was not about the technical aspect of his actions but the ethical one. My next question would have to be very explicit.

"Look, Leibele, don't you think it's wrong to forge someone else's signature?"

Leibele was really surprised. Apparently, it had never occurred to him that there might be something seriously wrong about what he had done. He was silent for most of the way home, and I got the impression that he was having an inner struggle.

After awhile, he turned to me and said, "Look, when you put it that way, I can see that there might be some people who would consider it forgery. I mean, I did sign someone else's name. But so what?"

I was floored. I had already explained that what he had done was forgery, but if he didn't see what was wrong with that... Besides, I felt there was a limit to how much I could preach to Leibele, since his intention was to save me from so many unfair punishments. I decided to drop the matter for the time being.

"What do we tell our parents?" I asked Leibele.

"I was trying to come up with an idea, but you keep bothering me with distracting questions. Right now, I haven't the faintest idea what to do. Our parents will definitely not be pleased that we've been kicked out of *cheder*."

"Maybe we should just tell them the truth?" I suggested tentatively.

The expression on Leibele's face told me that he was alarmed at the foolishness of my risky idea. "The truth?" he echoed. "Do you know what that means?"

"Sure," I declared. "Once we tell them the whole story, I'm sure they'll believe me that I've been picked on unfairly and that you were just trying to save me."

Of course, that made no sense in Yerushalayim of those days. And if you ask me, while it's true that there were teachers who took advantage of the situation to treat students unfairly, for the most part, the *chinuch* was good and real. Strict, but good and real, with lots of *simchah* and true devotion.

Leibele decided to deviate from his usual custom and tell the truth. Astonishingly enough, our parents, against all expectations, did indeed believe us, and in the end, they decided to transfer us to a different Talmud Torah.

All this is just an introduction to the story I want to tell you. The purpose of this introduction was to demonstrate Leibele's personality as a troublemaker with an incomparably good heart, and also to underscore the close bond we shared.

Even when Leibele was in his nineties, I could see the mischievousness peeking out through his beard and his wrinkles, though I never pointed it out to anyone else — or even to Leibele, for that matter.

One morning a number of years ago, Leibele told me, "I need you, my friend, to sign my second will."

This statement was somewhat confusing.

The Will

First of all, since when does a "Tchalmer" write a will? Did he have anything to bequeath to his children? I knew that Leibele, like me, owned no assets. Even his house didn't really belong to him; it belonged to the *kollel* of Batei Ungarin, and we both knew that once he passed away, it would be given to a waiting young couple even before they'd had a chance to bury him. Besides, we had always been taught that it was best to leave one's children nothing but debt, because that way we could be sure they wouldn't fight over it...

So why was he talking about a will?

Second of all, Leibele never had any children, so to whom would the will be addressed?

Third of all, a *second* will? When had he written a first will?

Leibele assured me that indeed, he had no assets and affirmed that he didn't have to whom to bequeath the assets he lacked. He just wanted to write down some ideas he'd come up with for the benefit of the coming generations, along with bits of advice he'd heard from his parents.

Besides, Leibele told me, the matter of the first will was giving him no rest, because he wasn't happy about what was written there and also because no one had signed it. "I think the real reason I want to write a second will is to erase the memory of the first will, which was written many years ago," he said. "That's why the very first paragraph will be that all previous wills I've written are null and void."

Understandably, this all sounded very mysterious to me. "I'm ready and willing to sign your will," I told him, "but first you've got to satisfy my curiosity and tell me when you wrote the first will."

"Oh," he replied, "that happened many years ago. Do you remember Yossel, 'the living-dead man'?"

"Of course I do," I told him. "but 'Yossel, the living-dead

man,' became the 'dead-dead man' when we were twenty years old, isn't that right?"

"It is," Leibele agreed, reminding me of the affair that many people in Meah Shearim — at least those who lived there seventy years ago — will never forget.

Yossel "the living dead-man" was a relatively wealthy man, at least by the standards of Jerusalemites, in general, and those living Meah Shearim, in particular. He owned a number of successful businesses and lived in a nice house. He had beautiful children who were always well dressed and who did well in school.

When his oldest son became of marriageable age, it soon became apparent that Yossel was suffering from a strange condition that didn't even have a name.

Yossel turned down every single *shidduch* suggested for his son, and believe me, the very best girls from Yerushalayim and other cities were suggested. It was obvious that he barely listened to the name before waving his hand in dismissal.

At first, people thought that perhaps his older son suffered from a problem the family had somehow managed to keep secret, but the same scenario repeated itself when *shadchanim* began suggesting matches for his daughter, who had reached marriageable age as well. Every suggestion was immediately ruled out by Yossel, no matter which yeshivah the boy studied in, what type of *bachur* he was, or what type of family he came from.

The years passed and the younger children, too, reached marriageable age and then became older singles. At the turning point of our story, all of Yossel's children were between the ages of 28-40, and unmarried.

The Will

The situation grew progressively worse because Yossel didn't make do with rejecting proposals. He became angry with people who made suggestions, complaining that they were insulting him and his children with their inappropriate suggestions.

Why, you might ask, didn't Yossel's children do anything about the situation? Apparently, they were emotionally incapable of withstanding their father's pressure. No one knows how Yossel managed to convince his children that he had only their best interests at heart, but the dismal situation spoke for itself: Yossel's eight children were getting older and older and their father, who could have been enjoying a clan of grandchildren, was missing out on all that *nachas* because of his stubborn foolishness.

At some point, a group of people formed a committee to solve the problem of Yossel's children. They informed the *gedolim* of the situation, hoping that they would wield their considerable influence over Yossel. Sadly, they all withdrew from the matter after a few attempts, seeing that he would not be swayed. "He's like a living dead-man," one of the *gedolim* sighed. From then on, Yossel was known as "the living dead-man."

And then Yossel did the noblest thing a father like him could do for his children.

He died.

Just like that, he sat down one fine day to drink a glass of tea, and then suddenly reconsidered and died.

Never had there been such a *levayah* in Yerushalayim until then and never was there such a *levayah* thereafter — not because of the amount of people who attended, but because of their happy mood.

Unpleasant as it is to admit, with the exception of Yossel's wife and children, those who attended the *levayah* had to control themselves, lest they burst into song or break into a dance. Everyone was smiling, and comments such as "finally," "it's about time," and "now *that* was considerate of him," were exchanged without a trace of irony.

If Yossel's death was tumultuous news, his will was even more so.

"My dear children," Yossel had written. "I request your forgiveness that I caused you to remain unmarried for so long. I've recently begun to fear that it was the wrong thing to do, but my pride did not allow me to change after so many years. Therefore, I asked Hashem to take my soul so that you might be able to marry. Now I order each of you to hurry and accept the first *shidduch* suggested by a reputable *shadchan*, and from *Shamayim* I will merit seeing you celebrate weddings and embrace children for years to come."

Word of the will spread and everyone wanted to see it. Indeed, with the family's consent, the will was taken to the shop of "the Romanian photographer" on Rechov Yechezkel and duly photographed. It was passed from hand to hand and everyone praised Yossel, the living dead-man, who, in his death, had finally granted his children freedom.

A day after the *shloshim*, Yossel's son got engaged. The other children followed in quick succession, with a two-week break between one engagement and the next. As difficult as it was for them to get engaged during Yossel's lifetime, that's how simple it was after his passing, thanks to his will.

The children, who had always obeyed their father's word implicitly, did so after his passing as well. They all married the first *shidduch* suggested to them by a reputable *shadchan*, paying no attention, of course, to all the jokesters who tried their luck.

The Will

Due to their advanced age, Yossel's children all had brief engagements. Within half a year, all his children were married, and two weeks before Yossel's first *yahrtzeit,* his oldest son celebrated the birth of a son, who was, of course, named Yossel.

Yossel's family grew and grew, and today, seventy years later, it numbers more than a thousand people, with many Yossels among them.

That's the story of Yossel, the "living dead-man." I would never have remembered to tell you this story had my friend Leibele not reminded me of it seventy years after Yossel's passing.

I thought Leibele was trying to use the story as a diversionary tactic, and I was having none of it. "Leibele," I told him, "I definitely remember that story, but you didn't answer the question of why you wrote a first will in your youth."

Leibele looked at me and said, "You know, it's not like you not to put two and two together." He paused. "On second thought, maybe it is like you. When we were children, you couldn't understand how I could have written the notes that saved you from the *menahel.*"

I truly felt Leibele was trying to confuse me. "What does the *menahel* have to do with your first will?" I asked. "And why do you want to write a second one?"

Understanding dawned even before I finished my sentence.

"It was you!" I exclaimed. "You wrote Yossel's will! *Oy,* how did I fail to realize that?"

Leibele smiled, and for the first time, admitted his big secret.

"When they announced Yossel's *levayah*, I had the same reaction as everyone else. I breathed a sigh of relief in the knowledge that his children would finally be able to marry. But then I suddenly began to worry. If Yossel had such a hold over his children that he was able to prevent them from marrying even once they were mature adults, who was to say that they wouldn't think, out of a misguided sense of loyalty, that they had to do his will even after his passing?

"So when everyone went to the *levayah*, I entered Yossel's home through the joint attic shared by all the Batei Ungarin homes. I sat at Yossel's desk, looked at a few *chiddushei Torah* he'd written, picked up his pen, and wrote that will. I knew that it would accomplish two things: cleanse poor Yossel's name somewhat, and even more importantly, he would merit to have grandchildren to carry on the family name.

"That was my first will; now do you understand why I want to write a second?"

Moved beyond words, I signed as a witness to his second will.

Why am I telling this story today?

Because my friend Leibele passed away a few weeks ago. Although he and his wife were childless, they never considered divorcing. Twenty years ago, she passed away and he was left alone.

When he passed away, I had reason to fear that there would be a poor showing at his *levayah*.

I decided I had to do something. I went to Zupnik (a central *shteibel* in Yerushalayim), spoke to the right people, and made sure the matter was respectably publicized. A few thousand people showed up! I especially made sure that Yossel's

The Will

family and offspring should be there. I told them to come because I would be publicizing something very important.

When the time came for *hespedim* to be delivered at the open grave, I told everyone about Leibele's first will, which had resulted in Yossel's having thousands of grandchildren, great-grandchildren and great-great-grandchildren.

"As you know, Leibele died childless," I told them. "I'm sure that he knew that forgery was a form of deceit and is therefore strictly forbidden — except in certain cases where Chazal allow it, such as '*mipnei darkei shalom*,' because of the ways of peace. So I want to say two things in his defense," I said.

"First of all, he did this when he was still a young man — 'A child can disguise himself with his deeds,' the *pasuk* in *Mishlei* says, 'but your end shall increase exceedingly.' Secondly, the forgery was carried out with completely noble intentions. What Leibele did was pretty close to '*mipnei darkei shalom*.' The fact is that his writing the will prevented the perpetuation of a terrible situation and accomplished much good. So many children were born thanks to his intervention! I say we can only envy his merit."

And all of Yerushalayim, young and old, wiped away a tear for Leibele, whose forged will had resulted in the blossoming of an entire family that had almost been severed.

Who Is a Champion

A ba'al teshuvah and his family move to a city suited to their new lifestyle.

One of his new neighbors is a quarrelsome, confrontational sort of fellow who has already caused a number of residents to move out of the area.

This time, though, he finds he's up against someone who does not respond to his barbs and certainly never stoops to fighting with him.

In the end, there was no escaping a confrontation, which changes the entire picture...

I live in a *chareidi* city in central Israel and my neighborhood is populated by longstanding, deep-rooted, very conservative *chareidi* families.

Approximately three years ago, a "different" family moved to our block. The man wore a large yarmulke but was clean-shaven; his wife covered her hair with a kerchief — in short, *ba'alei teshuvah*.

I don't want to open the topic on how *ba'alei teshuvah* are treated in certain *chareidi* areas. In sharp contrast to peripheral cities, which are usually characterized by a spirit of openness and acceptance, *ba'alei teshuvah* living in Bnei Brak or Yerushalayim don't have an easy time of it, especially if they look obviously new to Judaism. In large *chareidi* areas, the neighbors' attitudes range from passive acknowledgment to complete indifference.

In our building there lived a man who was intolerant of anyone who was not exactly like him. He was hostile not only to Sephardim but also to Ashkenazim who didn't belong to his *kehillah*. He held a collective scorn for anyone who was different from him.

Since he was an aggressive person, no one confronted him. If he confronted you, you withdrew immediately. Every so often, he would pick a fight with a passerby who had parked his car in a way that was not to his liking, or with a family who had set down some shopping bags near his apartment for a few moments.

The building in which he lived was occupied only by those whom he found acceptable — not because he was lucky, but because he'd chased the others away. Still, he felt the need to argue with and insult anyone who was different from him. Members of my family were at the receiving end of his barbs on more than one occasion, but we never dared retaliate or even complain. The last thing we needed was for him to start a neighborhood smear campaign against us!

Now you understand why, when a *ba'al teshuvah* family moved in directly opposite the entrance to his building, the residents of nearby buildings regarded them sadly from behind their shutters. Everyone knew these people would suffer for a few months and then move away as fast as possible, even if that meant breaching their rental contract and losing money.

Not five minutes had passed before the man showed up with comments about the moving van being parked improperly, the movers who were destroying the building with their clumsy maneuvers, and, of course, a stream of insulting comments against the new neighbor. He issued strange warnings and hurled baseless accusations. For example, he warned the new neighbor not to bring a TV into his home. When the new neighbor explained that they had chosen this neighborhood precisely because none of the neighbors owned television sets, the quarrelsome neighbor made a complete turnaround and said, "You think no one here owns a TV? The houses here are full of them! You have nothing to look for here."

We followed the new fellow's reaction closely. Usually, the arguments began immediately, because our neighbor had a unique talent for making people lose their self-control.

The new tenant was different. He didn't seem like the type of guy you could step on, but he maintained his cool and did not respond to the neighbor's attempts to drag him into a fight.

He responded politely at first, and then, after a few minutes, regarded the troublemaker with a look that asked wordlessly: *What is this guy's problem?* After that, he simply did not respond, or he said, "Fine, will do," and things like that.

From that point on, the veteran neighbor began a campaign of harassment with the declared intent of causing the new neighbor to leave the building. In fact, the old neighbor said so explicitly within earshot of the new one. Every day he'd show up with new nasty comments or attempts to argue.

The man simply wanted to fight, and he usually achieved his desire, because when you want to chase someone away and you invest great *hishtadlus* toward that end — you're usually successful. Until now, anyone who had been the object of our problematic neighbor's harassment campaigns would suffer bitterly, try to fight back, and then realize that the situation would not improve. Once he would come to that realization, he would leave the area as quickly as possible.

◿ ◿ ◿

That is the reason the problematic neighbor was so sure of himself. Five families had already left; there was no reason this family should be any different. But months passed, and they stayed put.

He saw it as a personal affront. How could it be that neighbors he was harassing didn't want to leave, and weren't even deigning to fight with him? The nerve of them! He decided to step up his campaign.

The new neighbor was incomparably refined, and so were his wife and children. They would find bags of garbage near their door, and simply take them down to the garbage bin. Their car would be littered with sunflower seeds, and they would quietly remove them. We wondered about this behavior. The new neighbor didn't look like a wimp. He was tall and muscular, and his face radiated power and strength. Still, he behaved as if he were the old neighbor's personal servant. I couldn't understand why he was taking all this harassment sitting down.

He seemed calm, as if whatever was going on had nothing to do with him. Sometimes, I saw a spark of bewilderment in his eyes, or even disapproval, but he always tried to get along with the nasty neighbor, appeasing him with comments such as, "I understand, sir. It won't happen again. I'll speak to the children about being quiet. You're right."

I never saw the slightest hint of anger in him.

The old neighbor, on the other hand, was a master at annoying and irritating others. If there were to be a "getting on people's nerves" competition, there's no question he would have quickly been declared the national champion — no, make that the world champion. He really knew how to step on people's toes, and in most cases, he reached his goal within a very short time. After incessant goading, the object of his harassment would finally scream, threaten — even hit. At that point, the old neighbor would call the police. The other neighbors didn't dare tell the police that the old neighbor had been asking to get pushed (after blocking the doorway of the new neighbor's home, or placing an overturned garbage can near his door). As far as the police were concerned, when there was violence involved, the object of the neighbor's complaints was arrested for assault and battery. After an incident like that, it was just a matter of time before one of the local moving companies received new business: to move the "undesirable" family out of the neighborhood.

But this new neighbor simply did not show signs of anger and did not appear to even consider moving out. This increased the respect the other neighbors felt for him. Once, after a serious episode, some of them asked him how he put up with this type of abuse. "*Kapparas avonos*," the fellow replied. "Apparently, Hashem is testing me. I must withstand the *nisayon*."

One Shabbos, the *ba'al teshuvah*'s in-laws came to visit.

I don't know whether or not they were observant, but they were certainly not *chareidi*.

In middle of Shabbos, our neighbor attacked the new resident with a stream of hurtful words in the presence of

Who Is a Champion

his father-in-law. It was a terrible *chillul Hashem*. The guest looked into his son-in-law's eyes as if to say, *Is this how people here behave? Is this why you came here?* We were all ashamed, and for the first time, I saw what appeared to me to be a spark of anger in the new neighbor's eyes.

He did not respond, though, trying instead to appease the out-of-control neighbor with soothing words. "Sir, let's discuss this on Motza'ei Shabbos. This is my wife's father; let's accord him the respect he deserves."

"He couldn't possibly have known you before he let his daughter marry you," the neighbor said without missing a beat. "I would never allow my daughter to marry someone like you."

At this point, two neighbors couldn't bear it anymore and intervened. Turning to the guest, they praised his son-in-law warmly. "You have a diamond of a son-in-law," they told him, "a treasure. He is so refined! He's the only one who controls himself and never yells back at this awful neighbor." They described some of the abuse he was going through and praised the son-in-law, lest his father-in-law believe any of the neighbor's accusations.

The old neighbor was shocked to see the other neighbors stand up to him. Cursing roundly, he wheeled around and returned home. The neighbors told the son-in-law that they saw his suffering and deeply admired the way he constantly controlled himself. They suggested that perhaps the time had come for him to respond. The son in-law, hurt and upset, did not respond to these suggestions. Instead, he merely thanked the neighbors for sticking up for him. Obviously, their support made the situation a bit easier for him to deal with. He said he would think about it after Shabbos.

On Motza'ei Shabbos, the new neighbor made *havdalah*, said goodbye to his in-laws. He prepared himself, knowing that it was only a matter of time until the old neighbor came over to speak with him.

I had a very uneasy feeling about what would happen next. I had known the old neighbor for many years and I knew that he was a tough person who never gave a thought to other people's considerations or feelings, never mind actually understand them. I also knew that for he first time, the new neighbor actually felt very angry. This was the moment the old neighbor had been waiting for. I was expecting the worst.

From the window of my house, I could see the neighbor waiting patiently. From afar, I heard a shout. I glanced down the street and saw a few street youths surround the problematic neighbor, yelling and cursing.

I'm not sure what happened. Perhaps he told them something that angered them, or perhaps they called out to him and he responded in that unique way of his. Either way, he was now in deep trouble.

The new neighbor, who was waiting for his harasser, also noticed that something was going on at the other end of the street. At first, he ignored it, because it didn't involve him, but then he realized that someone was being attacked. He ran over quickly and called out, "What's going on here?"

"Butt out! It's none of your business!" they told him.

Then he saw the awful neighbor at the center of it all. "Guys, he's older than you," he said to the street youths. "I'm warning you to leave him alone."

His voice was sharp and authoritative, not at all like the submissive, appeasing, refined voice we were used to hearing. He spoke as if he were accustomed to dealing with juvenile delinquents.

One of the youths turned to him and said rudely, "Get out of here! Why are you butting in to our business?"

Who Is a Champion

But the new neighbor didn't spare him so much as a glance, because the other two thugs had thrown the older man to the ground and had begun kicking him.

I can't explain what happened, but in an instant, the two thugs had been hurled onto the hood of a nearby parked car. The new neighbor, refined and polite as always, had flung them over without half trying.

The two others saw what happened and rushed over. One of them tried to throw a punch just as the other attempted to deliver a well-placed kick, but the new neighbor deflected the blows and pinned the second set of thugs to the same parked car he'd flipped their buddies onto.

The elderly neighbor was lying on the ground, watching in utter amazement as the youths regrouped and charged at the new neighbor. They were absolutely furious! The *ba'al teshuvah*, his facial expression indifferent, pushed them away with a few sharp movements, and before they knew what had hit them, they were all sprawled out on the floor.

"Are you okay?" the *ba'al teshuvah* asked the neighbor on the ground, extending a hand to help him up while simultaneously throwing a quick, neat punch to deflect two of the thugs who had risen to their feet and lunged at him once again.

At this point, six street youths from a nearby corner joined the fray. It seemed as if they would soon be reciting *Kaddish* for the young man, but astonishingly enough, he stood his ground with amazing calm, and whoever drew near him found himself on the floor. It was incredible. With quick hand-motions, well-placed kicks, and neat deflections, our submissive, obedient neighbor — who had been mistreated for so many months by a man who was now attempting to stagger to his feet — was fighting off ten thugs and doing a good job of it, too!

As he fought the thugs, he somehow managed to move the elderly neighbor aside so he wouldn't get hurt.

Interestingly, he was not enraged or vindictive. It was obvious that he was not seeking to inflict any pain; he was merely defending himself. He had not an ounce of fear as he focused intently on two goals: protecting the neighbor and defending himself.

At this point, a crowd had gathered, which increased the thugs' desperation to regain their lost honor. They withdrew for a moment to plan an organized attack on the fellow who was creaming them, believing that if they worked together in an organized fashion, they could overcome him.

The eight of them who could still walk closed in on him menacingly. He warned them that if they came any nearer, chances were they'd require medical treatment. A moment later, they were all on the floor, wailing in pain and calling their friends for backup.

At this point, the *ba'al teshuvah* took his neighbor by the arm and said, "Let's go home."

"Running away, are you?" one of the thugs shouted. "What a coward!"

They laughed, but the *ba'al teshuvah* did not even deign to respond. It was obvious that he hoped the incident was over. He had no desire for victory. All he'd wanted, when he first stepped in, was to save his neighbor.

The two were walking toward their building when a car suddenly screeched to a stop. Four thugs, friends of the previous gang, stepped out. They were holding iron crowbars. The *ba'al teshuvah* pushed the elderly neighbor into the yard of one of the buildings, told him to run, and turned to face the four attackers.

They closed in on him and within a minute, two of them

were on the floor, their weapons in the *ba'al teshuvah*'s hands. He stood facing the other two. After few seconds of silence he tossed the crowbars to the floor and said, "I'm unarmed. Want to fight? I'm game, but perhaps you should find out first what happened here."

One of the thugs, the leader, stepped forward and cried out, "Hey, aren't you Avi Cohen (fictitious name)?"

"That's me."

"I don't believe it. You mean you've become a *ba'al teshuvah*?"

"It's been three years now, *baruch Hashem*."

"Forgive me, Avi, I didn't know it was you. Do you know whom we're fighting?" he said to his friends, who were gathering around him, as they attempted to nurse their injuries. "This is Avi Cohen, the national boxing champion."

He began enumerating all the medals Avi had won at the Olympics and at world championship tournaments. The gang's demeanor changed instantly, as they began shaking the new neighbor's hand and asking his forgiveness. He treated them all kindly, but reprimanded them for trying to harm an elderly person.

The matter ended with embraces and handshakes.

The thugs dispersed, leaving only the elderly neighbor, who had left his hiding place in the yard as soon as he'd sensed that the danger was over. Apparently, he'd heard the thugs' revelation regarding the man he'd abused over the past year, and even if he hadn't, he'd seen with his own eyes what all of us had seen.

They stood facing each other and the elderly neighbor asked, "Tell me, why didn't you say anything all this time?"

"I want to run away from that era of my life. Why should I talk about it? It's not something I'm proud of."

PEOPLE SPEAK 5

"But I didn't deserve that you should defend me," he said.

"It's okay, Reb Yid. Let's put it behind us, okay?" Suddenly he paused, reconsidered and said, "The truth is, you wanted to discuss something with me. But there's no need anymore, is that right?"

"No need," the neighbor hurriedly agreed.

🕮   🕮   🕮

I'm sure it's superfluous to mention that our elderly neighbor no longer harasses anyone, certainly not this particular neighbor. Whenever I think about this story, I'm amazed anew at the powerful lesson it teaches.

Here was a man who left fame and glory for *Yiddishkeit*. He'd been a fighter for years, yet he was able to ignore harassment that would have provoked any ordinary person to resort to his fists. Even more amazing is that he chose to hide a fact that could have resolved the situation the moment it became known. The reason he controlled himself was that he truly wanted to withstand the test Hashem was giving him.

The *ba'al teshuvah*'s children are students in the finest schools in our city. He is beloved by the entire neighborhood, most of all by his former enemy, who has had a complete change of heart.

When I think of the period during which he tried so hard to appease his neighbor, I realize that he was a champion of a different sort, as well — the kind we all strive to become.

"Who is strong? He who overcomes his inclination."

Nursing Home

An elderly widower, the head of a large family, makes the decision to live in a nursing home even though his children would be glad to have him live with them.

The problem is that they are not willing to put up with his second wife.

This is a story about people who want to honor their parent, but only under certain conditions...

I'm writing to you from my room in the nursing home where I've been a resident for the past few years.

I saw in your previous book that you featured letters from elderly people, so I decided to write to you as well.

The truth is that I've been meaning to write for quite some time already, but somehow I never got around to it. Then, an amusing incident occurred here at the nursing home, and that pushed me to write.

One day, we saw a notice on the bulletin board in the nursing home that at a particular time on particular date, we would hear a story from Chaim Walder.

Of course, many residents of the nursing home, myself

included, called our children so they would tell the grandchildren to come hear the story. The truth is that our real intention was to use the story as a pretext to get the children to come visit. We know that they can't always find the time for us, but for a story…

When the big day arrived, we hurried to grab seats half an hour before the scheduled time. You may not be aware of this, but elderly people sometimes behave like first graders, arguing over seats as if their lives depended on them.

It was 7:30 P.M. The dining room was full of elderly people, their adult children and lots of little kids who had come especially to hear you tell a story.

And then… a young girl entered the room. She sat down at the table laid with a tablecloth and a pitcher of water, opened your book and said, "*A Son for a Son*. A story by Chaim Walder."

◆   ◆   ◆

She couldn't understand why there was an angry buzz in the room. "Do you know the story already?" she asked.

"We thought the author himself was coming to tell the story," someone shouted by way of explanation.

Only after some discussion did we understand that no one in the management had ever dreamed of bringing you in. It was just that the notice was phrased in a way that was unintentionally misleading. The poor girl read the story, and we all listened — even though we know it practically by heart — but we had a hard time hiding our disappointment. Poor girl.

This happened quite recently. I'm telling you about it in the hope that you might decide to set things right and come tell us a story. It would have to be on a purely volunteer basis, because the managers of our nursing home prefer to pay

Nursing Home

a young girl a few dollars rather than spend real money on us. It's a real *nebach* on them. How can we ask them to dip into their pockets and withdraw more than a few bucks?

If you detect a note of bitterness on my part, just ignore it. It's part of life at the nursing home, I think.

I realize that I've hurled you into a world with which you're not familiar, that of elderly people who have already lived through everything they needed to endure in life. I would put it this way: We are "people whose future is already behind them."

The truth is that the world of the elderly is not that different from the world of the young. We have all the same struggles as the young — a difficult financial situation, competition, jealousy, comparisons between ourselves and others — only we must deal with these situations under more difficult circumstances. Our health is shaky; our bodies betray us; we feel detached from the younger generation. We struggle with the feeling that life has passed us by; we feel intense disappointment over the way our once-beautiful life is ending — and most of all, we're terrified of the inevitable ending.

Add to all that the fact that an elderly person no longer has the strength for pretense the way he did when he was younger. At this point, it's simply not worth the effort to try and impress others with refined behavior. What's left is the basic *middos* that a person worked on during his lifetime.

All the less-than-beautiful character traits people go to great lengths to conceal throughout their lifetime now gain expression. Someone who craved honor but managed to conceal that craving — won't bother hiding it anymore. Angry people won't restrain themselves. Envious people will make no secret of their jealousy and crude people will stop watching their language.

Truly refined people, on the other hand, will be revealed in their true glory. People who truly rejoiced in others' good fortune will continue to radiate love and goodness to those around them. People who were truly dignified and gracious throughout their lives won't hassle the nursing home staff all the time, choosing instead to suffer in silence.

So as I said, the nursing home is a type of laboratory with controlled conditions that expose the real nature of human beings.

You may be wondering why I'm in a nursing home and not in my own home.

I know the elderly sometimes say that their children "locked them away" in a nursing home. Perhaps this was the right choice of words in the past, but nowadays, I must say, many elderly people prefer living in a nursing home to living at home, because practically speaking, a nursing home is much like a hotel. People enjoy staying at a hotel because they are provided with meals, there's good company, and even entertainment. The same is true for a nursing home, or an "assisted-living retirement home," as they are often called.

Elderly people need company even more than young people do, because they are not in the work force anymore. The elderly, even those whose children honor them greatly, tend to suffer from acute loneliness.

I don't mean to make a sweeping generalization, but that's how it is for most people.

The nursing home provides essential services and keeps us busy with interesting activities. Yes, sometimes they promise us Chaim Walder and end up sending a young girl to read a story he wrote, but that really was our mistake. Besides, there was something positive about the experience: It gave us lots of material for grumbling about the management, and that's

Nursing Home

part of the fun, too — at least for some of us at the nursing home. But the reason I'm in the nursing home is completely different.

❦ ❦ ❦

I was married to my first wife for more than fifty years. We had seven children, married them off in a respectable fashion, and kvelled when the grandchildren started coming in quick succession. Life was wonderful.

Then my wife was diagnosed with the dreaded disease. I accompanied her throughout her difficult journey, watching her deteriorate in front of my eyes, until the bitter end. When her eyes closed forever, she was surrounded by her beloved husband and children.

Chazal tell us that a woman's loss is felt most acutely by her husband. I experienced this on my own flesh, especially since we'd shared a truly wonderful bond.

I was devastated. My life held no meaning. I withdrew into my house and rarely went out. To my children's credit, they came to visit me and invited me to their houses all the time. They really treated me with utmost respect.

After three years of loneliness and much persuasion by others, I agreed to try and begin a new chapter in my life. After a few unsuitable suggestions, the name of a woman, who had been widowed seven years earlier, came up. We met a few times and decided to marry.

My second wife brought much happiness into my life. True, she was very different from my first wife, but I have a very open nature and can form an emotional connection with any type of person. I found her to be a wonderful wife. After three years of difficult loneliness, I was finally alive again, in all aspects of the word.

But when it came to my children, the relationship was doomed from the start.

❦ ❦ ❦

I can't put my finger on the reason, but even before we married each of my children in turn had an argument with her. They discussed her supposed shortcomings with one another and eventually began treating her with open hostility. They even tried to convince me not to marry her.

I blamed my oldest daughter, who is today herself a grandmother. She behaved the way young orphans sometimes behave when they can't accept the fact that someone is taking the place of a deceased parent — ignoring, rebelling and lashing out.

I didn't think this could happen with adults, but I was wrong. In fact, it's worse with an adult, because adults have the power and brains to be really vicious.

My daughter didn't stop at merely hating my wife. She persuaded all my other children to despise her as well. The situation reached a point where my children mocked her, ignored her when they ran into her in the street, and found seemingly unlimited ways to cause her indescribable pain.

These were my children, whom I knew to be good, well-raised and wonderful in *every* way!

At one point, my children managed to convince me that my wife had behaved improperly on a certain occasion. I made a comment to my wife about the matter. Her reaction was swift and terrible: she told me she was leaving — and she did.

❦ ❦ ❦

I sat at home, lonely and sad. I cried for days and nights

Nursing Home

and then I called her and pleaded with her to come back. I never would have believed I was capable of doing something like that, but I felt my life was not worth living without her.

At first, she responded coldly and refused to listen. Then she agreed on condition that we go to counseling.

So, at age seventy-six, we went to a marriage counselor.

The counselor spoke to my children (who all had families of their own) both as a group and individually, trying to rectify the situation. He was not successful.

Then he spoke to me. "You're trapped," he said to me. "You have to choose between her and your children. It won't work any other way. Your children are all blindly following your oldest daughter. She has a very dominant nature and she's pulling them all in her direction. They really think you married an evil woman."

"What do you think?" I asked.

"I think that never has such a regal, special woman come to me for counseling. Your children are the problem, not her. Your wife tried to be friendly and gracious. On more than one occasion, she swallowed her pride to keep the peace, but your children were determined to hate her. It's incredible. I've met people who care only about their own feelings and pay no attention to others, but I've never met such intelligent people who absolutely refuse to listen to reason. It's not as if they're irrational people; their stubbornness seems to be limited to this one area. You need to choose."

"What do you advise me to choose?" I asked.

"It's a tough call," he said. "Your wife is obviously important to you. Yet, on the other hand, you have seven children and dozens of grandchildren. I don't know if you can bear to give them up."

Three days later, I had made my decision.

I phoned my wife and invited her out to eat. I sat with her and told her openly what the counselor had said. I described the difficult decision I'd had to make.

"Well, which of us did you choose?" she asked, her voice strained.

"I choose you," I replied. "I'm at peace with my decision. My children will get along fine without me; I've given them everything they need. Now I need to think about myself."

"But thinking about yourself means maintaining contact with your children."

"That's why it took me three days to reach my decision that when all is said and done, you're the one who brings me joy. I'll never be able to give you up."

My wife wept with emotion. When she finished drying her eyes, she said, "But you know, no matter how your children behave, we can't manage without them."

It was true. My sons, daughters-in-law and daughters had very devotedly provided us with warm meals, helped me take my medication and monitored my medical care very closely. I couldn't deny that. I wasn't in the best of health and I needed their help.

I told her about the idea I'd come up with at some point during the past three days. "I'll sell our apartment and we'll go live in a nursing home where we'll be provided with meals and enjoy good medical care. We'll grow old together undisturbed."

She agreed immediately and that's the reason we're here in the nursing home. It's been ten years now, and we are indeed happily growing old together.

My wife and I are not healthy, but we're well cared for

Nursing Home

here. All our needs are seen to and we're kept busy with all types of activities, such as listening to your stories read aloud by a sixteen-year-old girl.

Surprisingly enough, my children come visit us from time to time. They felt very bad about my decision, but once I had made up my mind, there was no changing it. They accepted the situation and today they're trying to patch up what they destroyed. They treat my wife with respect. They don't dare be rude to her anymore.

That's my story, young man, and I'm sure many fathers and children will make personal use of it.

You know what?

If you really want to surprise me, come to the nursing home and speak to us seniors — for free, of course. Yes, you heard me. Am I being too pushy? That's okay at my age. Come over and tell any story you want.

Wait a minute. Except this one, of course.

5

The Fateful Farher

A talented, learned boy goes on a shidduch meeting. His intention, however, is not to meet the girl, but rather to confront her father.

The father, a learned Torah scholar in his own right, has a reputation for embarrassing every bachur who comes to meet his daughter by posing questions in learning so tough and challenging that everyone fails his test.

The hero of our story is sent by his friends to put the father in his place and give him a taste of his own medicine.

What happens next presents them both with a test...

My story took place more than twenty years ago, and I'm still hesitant about sharing it.

Despite my hesitations, I've decided to go ahead because it's a fascinating story and it teaches a very important lesson.

I was a student at one of the most well-known and distinguished yeshivos in Eretz Yisrael. This yeshivah boasted a concentration of the sharpest, most talented *bachurim* in the country. It was exceedingly difficult to be accepted to this yeshivah.

The Fateful Farher

Demand, as you surely know, causes value to increase. *Bachurim* who sense that their value has risen permit themselves to behave somewhat differently from those who are nervous about finding a good match. This behavior is completely unjustified and doesn't say much about their *middos*. Some of these *bachurim* dismiss perfectly suitable *shidduch* suggestions because their heads are so "up in the clouds" that their feet are simply not on the ground.

But that's not what my story is about.

📧   📧   📧

One of the *bachurim* at my yeshivah received a very impressive *shidduch* suggestion, a girl whose father held a distinguished Torah position.

He made some inquiries about her and heard very favorable information, so he agreed to a meeting.

When he arrived at the house, he was ushered into the dining room, where he waited for the date to begin.

But instead of the girl, it was her father who entered the room.

Tucked under his arm was a *gemara*, the *gemara* that the *bachurim* were learning in yeshivah at the time. The girl's father sat down and began testing him.

The *bachur* was shocked, but he didn't dare protest. For the next half hour, his prospective father-in-law grilled him on the *sugya*.

While it is considered perfectly acceptable to "talk in learning" on such occasions, this was an altogether different story. This was an *attack* in learning.

Every *yeshivah bachur* knows what it's like to be attacked in learning. It's not real and it's not *leshem Shamayim*; its only point is to show you how worthless you are. Most *bachurim* never have to deal with situations like this in *shidduchim*, and this boy had no idea how to get out of the awful spot in which he found himself.

At some point, he wanted to get up and say, "Excuse me, sir, this meeting is over. I don't think this *shidduch* has any potential," but of course he didn't dare.

After half an hour of torture, the real meeting began. The girl was truly special and the *bachur* thought her an extremely suitable match.

At the end of the evening, the *bachur* was thoroughly confused. On the one hand, he was very interested in a second meeting with the girl. But on the other hand, her father...

He returned to yeshivah and related what had happened. We, of course, advised him to drop the *shidduch*, but he said the girl was worth the terrible "entrance exam."

The girl's parents spared him the dilemma. Their answer was negative. The *shadchan* told him that the girl would have liked to meet him again, but her father had said a firm no.

We understood.

The truth is that had the response been positive, in my opinion the *bachur* wouldn't have gone through with it in any case, nor would any student in our yeshivah have accepted the suggestion thereafter.

But their answer was negative, and do you know what happens in such a case?

The value increases.

Hers, not ours.

⁂

She was suggested for a different *bachur* from the yeshivah, who received a heads-up about the *farher* he could expect.

The Fateful Farher

He prepared the way he had prepared before applying to *yeshivah gedolah*, studying the *sugya* thoroughly, but the scene repeated itself. The father attacked him in learning, presenting contradictions and refutation for everything he said and making him seem like a complete ignoramus.

This was a *bachur* who was very proud of the number of suggested matches he had turned down, but this time, he told the *shadchan* he was definitely interested in the *shidduch*. His enthusiasm, of course, was the result of the same theory that had caused him to turn down others...

However, the girl's father had not been impressed, and he told the *shadchan* that they were not interested in continuing.

At this point, the family's chances should have been finished — at least in our yeshivah — but it soon became apparent that the story had only just begun.

The *shidduch* became extremely desirable. Many *bachurim* went to special lengths to arrange to have their name suggested to the girl's family. It became a sort of competition: who was good enough to satisfy this tough-to-please father? You have to understand that these *bachurim* were all extremely proud of themselves; they felt as if they owned the world — and suddenly, their friends were being creamed, one after the other. Satisfying this man became a challenge at which everyone was eager to try his hand. Personally, I think it was boundless *ga'avah* and poor *middos* that made everyone think he would win.

But this father was very tough to win over. Every *bachur* who showed up at his house left feeling smaller than small. No one could tolerate this man's behavior, and yet, more and more *bachurim* kept trying.

I didn't even try.

I told everyone that I wasn't interested in such a *shver*, that I'd already taken my entrance exams before entering yeshivah and had no intention of going through another one — certainly not in the home I wanted to build.

The name was suggested for me a number of times, but I always responded firmly in the negative.

After about a year during which the family kept sending *shadchanim* to try to convince me to agree to a meeting, I finally gave in.

The family thought that I had finally caved in to their pressure — or perhaps that I had reached the conclusion that they were suitable for me, after all — but the truth was entirely different. I feel very uncomfortable admitting this, but what happened was that I caved in to the pressure that my friends had been putting on me. You see, one of my good friends had tried his luck with this *shidduch* and been thoroughly humiliated by the father. For quite some time, my friends had been begging me to agree to a meeting in order to put the father in his place.

At this point, I must explain, with all due modesty, that I was always a top learner. During *shiur klali*, I often had deep arguments in learning with the *rosh yeshivah*, so the *bachurim* were aware of the scope of my knowledge and my unusual capabilities.

They wanted me to go there and show him up in return for the humiliating tests to which he'd subjected all the *bachurim* before me.

At first, I didn't want to hear of it, but after my good friend was humiliated and terribly depressed as a result, I gave in to the pleas of the *bachurim* and told the *shadchan* who had been running after me for a few months that he could give the family a positive answer.

The Fateful Farher

I didn't even prepare for the test. I know that sounds arrogant, and I apologize, but I knew the *sugya* inside and out. I went with the intention of totally flattening the man.

And that's exactly what I did.

◆ ◆ ◆

He entered the room exactly as my friends had described, brimming with self-confidence. He tossed a question at me, but I didn't answer it. Instead, I asked him why he thought it was a question at all.

"Don't you see what Rashi says?" he asked me. "He completely contradicts the *gemara* on the previous page."

"You're obviously not familiar with the Rashi in *Bava Metzia*," I replied coolly. "If you had studied it, you would understand that your question is not even a question."

"What does Rashi say there?"

"Don't you remember?" I asked. "It's a Rashi on the well-known *sugya* of..." and I mentioned the name of that particular *sugya*.

He didn't remember the Rashi, and I let him squirm for awhile before quoting the first line of the Rashi. "Now do you remember?" I asked.

"Uh, can you go on a bit, another word or two?" he asked. I added one word, and then another, sounding as though I was talking to a fourth grader. Finally, he understood which Rashi I was referring to and why the question he had posed was not really a question at all.

"Very nice," he said, nodding approvingly. "That really clarifies this Rashi."

"It does? This Rashi is actually one of the hardest I've ever encountered."

"Why?"

"You're familiar with the *gemara* in *Kiddushin* on this topic, no?"

He said he was somewhat familiar.

"Well, that Rashi completely contradicts what Rashi says here."

I presented him with an explicit *gemara* that made the Rashi we were discussing seem most incomprehensible.

He tried suggesting a few explanations, but I refuted them all in a manner that made it clear to both of us that he didn't begin to know the *sugya*.

In the end, he admitted he didn't have an answer.

"I'm surprised," I said. "The *gemara* on this page resolves the problem." I pointed to and read aloud two lines from the *gemara* that clarified the entire matter.

Confused and perspiring, he said, "It's good, it's good... let me sit on that awhile. In the meantime, I think you should meet."

⁂ ⁂ ⁂

The truth is that at this point, I was faced with a problem. Putting a puffed-up peacock in his place is one thing, but meeting a girl for no reason is quite another. But it was too late. If I had left at this point, I would have shamed the girl. I went in.

She was the most special girl I had ever met, the complete antithesis of her father. Where he was tough, she was good. Where he was vain, she was modest. Where he was argumentative, she was refined and regal.

At the end of the meeting, I was thoroughly confused.

I didn't return to yeshivah. I was terribly mixed-up. I didn't know what to tell my friends.

I found myself waiting impatiently for an answer. I was sure

The Fateful Farher

it would be negative. I couldn't imagine that anyone would say yes to someone who had humiliated him like that.

◖   ◖   ◖

When the response came, I realized how wrong I was.
It was positive.
Now what did I tell the guys?
I returned to yeshivah and related that we'd had a "reasonable" argument in learning. I didn't describe what I had actually done, but I didn't pretend he had creamed me, either.

We met a number of times. Her father tried once more to engage me in a discussion about learning, and while the second time was not as traumatic as the first, it was sufficiently unpleasant to wean him off the idea of "starting up" with me again.

We got engaged (at the engagement, he tried "attacking" a few of my friends in learning); we married; and now we're marrying off our children.

Over the years, my father-in-law and I have had only a few learning "confrontations," and it always ended badly for him. For the most part, he avoids such confrontations with me, but I see him do it over and over again to his other sons-in-law, who have somehow managed to join the family. When this happens, I'm forced to defend them. Whenever he starts up with someone at the table, I intervene quickly and make him regret having done so. It has come to the point where the other sons-in-law prefer to come for Shabbos only if we are there, too; otherwise they'd be lynched in learning.

Today, years later, I'm writing this story with the purpose of discussing argumentativeness in learning.

Some people use the Torah "as a spade to dig with." I understand that for excellent scholars, it can be very tempting to engage in this sort of behavior and show off one's mental acuity and reasoning prowess. But aside from learning ability, a person needs *middos*, and *middos* ought to stop a person from behaving that way.

There are many ways to hurt a person's feelings, most of them obvious and overt, but with learning, it's done in secret. It looks like learning, but even a *lamdan* will tell you that learning it's not.

More than twenty years have passed, and I still feel guilty for the path that led to my *shidduch*. That "learning session" was definitely not *lishmah*. It's true that everything is *min ha-Shamayim*, but that still does not excuse what I did, which was basically a form of revenge.

I'd like to conclude with a good word about my father-in-law. There's something that may have escaped readers' attention, so I'd like to point it out explicitly: The fact that he was prepared to go ahead with the *shidduch* even after I humiliated him, highlights both his tremendous *ahavas haTorah* and his integrity. He may not have behaved fairly toward the other *bachurim*, but this was his way of letting them know how high he set the bar.

I think that my "performance" at our first meeting, which so impressed him, was really an indication of some not-so-impressive qualities. Luckily for me, he never realized that.

The Bodyguard

A security company receives an unusual mission: to guard a bride and groom on their wedding day.

If that were not surprising enough, they are shocked to learn the identity of the person posing the threat. At the wedding, the security guard begins to have doubts as to whether he's protecting the right people.

In the end, he receives his answer.

For quite some time now, I've been wanting to write to you about some of the interesting experiences I've had in my life, and believe me, I've had many.

I work as a bodyguard. People hire me to accompany them and protect them wherever they go. My fee ranges from $200–$500, depending on the nature of the job and the number of hours the subject requires my services.

Sometimes, the job I'm hired for carries minimal or no risk at all, while other times the risk is considerable. Some political figures require bodyguards even though their lives are not really in danger. The trouble is that every public personage has some enemies, and you never know when a mentally imbalanced individual might lash out at a public figure. Security does much to deter such people.

Famous celebrities often require protection for the opposite reason: mass admiration. These people can't even go to the grocery store without being descended upon by a horde of people clamoring for their autograph. Most people realize that they won't be able to get close to someone who has a bodyguard protecting him, and they will stay away; we've got to handle the small percentage of admirers who will try despite the odds.

Some people need bodyguards just because it makes the right impression. If you're an international businessman, you want to impress the people with whom you're meeting — two hulking bodyguards equipped with communication devices do a good job of that.

We understand our subjects' needs. Some clients want us to fade into the scenery as much as possible while others want us to put up a real show. We are always well aware of the reason we were hired, and try to do a good job at putting on an act, if necessary.

The story I want to tell you is about a strange assignment I once received. It taught me a lot about people's personalities and how they can sometimes ruin their own lives.

A secular couple arrived at our office and introduced themselves as the parents of a groom who was to marry in a week's time.

This was nothing new. I had already attended a number of weddings in the capacity of my job. In most cases, the clients were celebrities who wanted to keep out the press or any other uninvited guests. There were also some occasions

The Bodyguard

where people had reason to fear that someone would try and sabotage the event.

Securing weddings is a great job: the food is good and the atmosphere is pleasant.

I asked the groom's parents why they required security, and they said, "We don't need you to protect us. We want you to watch the bride's father."

"Why?" I asked.

"He might try and sabotage the wedding."

"Why would he do that?"

"Because he doesn't approve of the marriage," the father of the groom replied.

"How come?" I asked.

"Because she's marrying a *chareidi* fellow."

"Wait a minute," I said. "We're talking about your son, aren't we? You look completely secular."

"We are," the husband replied, "but our son became *chareidi* and we respect that."

"And the bride?"

"She, too, is from a secular home, but her father is not prepared to respect her choice," he replied.

He began telling a story so fascinating I never would have believed it had I not heard it with my own ears. The bride came from a broken family where all the children had, at one point or another, left home to live with foster families or with relatives. Their father had persecuted them and hurt them terribly.

"Our future daughter-in-law," he related, "left home at the age of sixteen to live with a foster family. After the father learned the identity of the family, she was spirited away to the home of a public personality and great pains were taken to keep her whereabouts a secret. At this point, she decided to participate in a *kiruv* seminar, after which she became a *ba'alas teshuvah*. A few years later, she got engaged to our son; and as soon as her engagement became public, her father heard about it and expressed his opposition to the marriage.

"He contacted us, the parents of the groom, and informed us that he was opposed to the match. We, who were only too well aware of what he was all about, pretended that we were opposed, as well — only what could we do? Our son wouldn't listen to us.

"When he heard this, he demanded that we join him in refusing to attend the wedding, but we told him that we had consulted with a psychologist who had advised us to respect our son's choices. We suggested that he, too, go to a psychologist but of course, he didn't take our advice.

"When he realized that the wedding would take place with or without him, he announced that he agreed to the wedding, but only on certain conditions.

"His 'conditions' were more or less equivalent to controlling the entire wedding: the hall, the food, the music — everything, basically. And he didn't even plan to contribute a cent; he hadn't done so for any of his other children and he wasn't about to start now.

"I informed him that he could hardly expect so much control over the wedding if he wasn't even paying part of the expenses. At that point, he began threatening us that he'd sabotage the wedding.

"That's why we're hiring you," he concluded.

The Bodyguard

For the first time, instead of protecting an individual from the masses, I had to protect the masses from an individual.

I was asked to stick to the father of the bride from the moment he arrived until the moment he left. I received clear instructions from the groom and his father that at the man's slightest attempt to create a problem, I was to escort him from the premises — using physical persuasion, if necessary.

The father of the bride was apprised of the situation. He was informed that he was invited to the wedding as a guest and would even be honored with a blessing under the *chuppah*, but that any attempt to sabotage the wedding or damage the joyous atmosphere would result in his immediate removal from the scene.

My partner and I arrived at four o'clock. I was curious to see what the subject looked like. I pictured him as a hulking fellow with a thick moustache. To my surprise, he looked like the type of person who wouldn't hurt a fly. He seemed very refined, with kind, soft eyes, a calm voice and a sincere smile on his lips. The father of the groom signaled us that this was our man. We couldn't believe it.

"Are you sure?" I asked him.

"One hundred percent," he responded.

We approached him, our manner courteous yet authoritative, and told him that from now until the end of the wedding, we would be following him wherever he went. He smiled a wistful smile that broke my heart and said, "Don't worry, I won't make any trouble. They must have painted me as a monster. The truth is that everything is completely the opposite of what they told you."

I told him that I respected him deeply, but that we had been hired by the people paying for the wedding, so we had to do our job and he had better cooperate.

PEOPLE SPEAK 5

He went to a table on the side of the hall and we followed him. We were dressed festively, like the other guests, and wore no communication devices or other dead giveaways. We did our best to appear natural so that it wouldn't be obvious to all the guests that the father of the bride was under close scrutiny. But in truth we didn't let him out of our sight for a moment.

᠆ ᠆ ᠆

We sat down on either side of him.

"I want you to hear my side of the story," he said to us. "I'm an upright fellow; I've never fought with a soul. I barely open my mouth. A few years ago, a couple of unscrupulous people took advantage of a difficult period I was going though to take my daughter away from me against my will. Not only that, they hid her whereabouts from us so we wouldn't know where to find her. She spent the next few years wandering from one home to another. You can't imagine how they brainwashed her. Once I bumped into her in the street. 'Please, come home,' I pleaded with her. 'We've never hurt you!' But she just looked at me coldly and walked right past me. We have a warm and loving home, and you should see where she ended up. Someone paid a couple of movers and shakers in the religious community a load of money and they arranged a match for her with a groom who is nowhere near as bright or as talented as she. I'm sitting here eating my heart out. Just think how you would feel if they were to take your son, feed him stories against you for years on end, and then you'd have to participate in his wedding with two bodyguards watching your every move."

The truth is that as a secular person, I began to sympathize with him.

"My wife has been crying in anguish and shame for

The Bodyguard

months. She misses her daughter so much. They're spreading lies about us, presenting us as violent people. You're welcome to check if I ever lifted a finger against anyone. Look at me. Do I look like the type of person who would sabotage a wedding? They just want to humiliate me."

He was right. He truly did not look like he could so much as break a plate, never mind ruin a wedding. I pitied him.

"It's okay, sir," I said. "Calm down. Your daughter's getting married; it's a happy occasion. No one will know we're bodyguards as long as you don't cause any trouble."

I truly empathized with the fellow. I was beginning to have my doubts as to who were the "good guys" and who were the "bad guys" in this story. I was afraid I'd been hired to humiliate a person whose daughter had been unjustly taken from him.

I'd never encountered such a dilemma before. True, a bodyguard projects a tough, uncaring image, but my job had never before forced me to hurt someone's feelings.

At the *chuppah*, the father of the bride stood alone, off to the side, weeping with emotion. He was honored with a blessing, and when he finished, I saw him whisper "*Mazal tov!*" to his daughter, who responded coldly. Anger welled up in my heart. With each passing moment, the feeling grew stronger that I was protecting the wrong people and hurting the wrong man.

🎬   🎬   🎬

After the *chuppah*, it was time for dancing. For the first time, I had to dance as part of my job. I'd fallen, crawled on my stomach, and even drawn a gun, but never had I danced on the job. I discovered that it was no easy feat. Aside from a few of the celebrants, no one knew what was going on. People must have wondered about the muscular men in middle of the circle, but no one volunteered any information.

At some point, the subject got tired of dancing and sat down. We sat down at his side. I felt so bad for him. He didn't deserve this type of treatment. He was not the type of person who needed to be watched like a hawk.

Apparently, he sensed how I felt. He placed a hand on my shoulder and said, "Thanks. You're the only person here giving me the strength to go through with this."

We sat in silence, and in my heart I felt a fierce desire to protect him and help him, only I couldn't think how.

Suddenly he said to me, "Did you see that?"

"What?" I asked.

He pointed to one of the guests sitting opposite us.

"That fellow," he said. "He just gave me a dirty look and formed a zero with his thumb and forefinger to show me exactly what he thought of me. He ought to be ashamed of himself, insulting a man at his daughter's wedding..."

This was too much. I went over to the person and said, "I'm going to have to ask you to leave at once."

"Why?" he asked.

"Because if you don't do so yourself, I'll have to help you. Aren't you ashamed to insult a man at his daughter's wedding?"

"I didn't do anything," the man replied. "He just can't stand my family."

I took him by the arm and began leading him out. "Leave me alone, I'll leave by myself," he said.

He began to leave, and I went back to where I'd left my subject.

He wasn't there.

The other security guard was nowhere to be seen, either.

The Bodyguard

I thought maybe they'd gone to dance, but I didn't see them anywhere on the dance floor.

I surveyed the hall, and suddenly I saw my partner confronting one of the guests. I hurried over and asked, "What are you doing?"

"The subject told me that you wanted me to remove this fellow because he'd angered him."

I didn't bother replying. "Where's our man?" I asked.

We both scanned the hall and came up blank. We divided the area into a few sections and checked each one carefully. Nothing. It was now clear as day that he was planning something.

Suddenly, the father of the groom approached me, accompanied by the man I had escorted outside. "What right did you have to ask a guest of mine to leave the wedding?" he asked, bristling. "Who's paying you, me or the father of the bride?"

"He said the man had insulted him."

"And you believed him?"

Suddenly, I realized that we were dealing with an extremely devious person. "Listen, I made a mistake, but the subject has disappeared. He must be up to no good!"

I sent the other guard to maintain eye contact with the bride. Then I took a deep breath and tried to think what I would do if I wanted to sabotage a wedding.

The father of the groom looked at me despairingly. "Do something," he pleaded.

"Give me a second," I replied. Suddenly, I knew where he would go. "The electricity!" I shouted. "Come with me!"

We ran to the office. We asked the maintenance man where the manager was and he said, "He went with the father of the bride."

PEOPLE SPEAK 5

I asked him where the main fuse box was, and he said it was on the second floor. I dashed up the stairs as fast as I could. From afar, I saw the owner of the hall opening the fuse box.

"Don't let him near that box!" I shouted, hurrying over. Out of the corner of my eye, I saw my subject reach for the box, but I lunged forward and shoved both the father of the bride and the owner to the side.

The owner of the hall was furious. "Are you crazy? I'm calling the police."

I held onto the subject and told the hall owner, "This man was planning to switch off the main switch to all the halls and sabotage his daughter's wedding. You're welcome to call the police."

"But he said there was a problem, that the lights were blinking."

"He lies very convincingly, but he's done for tonight. Is there a back exit?"

He showed me where to go. I lifted the subject and carried him as if he were an object. Outside, the other guard was waiting for me in a car. We sped off, the subject screaming, "How dare you! You're abducting me for no reason! I'm going to file a complaint against you! You'll never work as bodyguards again! I was just trying to help with the lights."

We didn't even respond. We just drove and drove for three-and-a-half hours, until were sure the wedding was over and the last of the guests had left.

The following morning, the couple called and thanked us for having prevented the tumult and chaos that could have ensued. "Knowing my father," said the bride, "he wouldn't have made do with merely switching off the electricity. That would be to easy to fix. He'd have found a way to ensure

The Bodyguard

that workers would spend two hours fixing the problem, only to then discover another one. You don't know him."

"I've never met such a misleading person," I admitted. "He managed to win me over to his side."

"I don't blame you. He did the same thing to me and to each of my siblings. The only solution was to cut off all contact. He's very persuasive and has a controlling personality. If that's what happened to you within an hour, think what kind of damage he did to us over the course of a few years."

"Did he hit you?" I asked.

"Never," the bride replied. "He never lifted a finger against us, but you saw for yourself that he doesn't need to. He simply pits people against each other. He would arrange for us to hurt one another and he would side sometimes with one of us and sometimes with the other. He abused us verbally and emotionally, causing us to argue with one another, hurting and humiliating us. He brought about a situation so tragic you'd rather not hear about it."

I was actually very interested.

I listened in shock as she described her life to me.

Her father suffered from borderline personality disorder. (His father — her grandfather — had been the same way.) After his marriage, he worked his "magic" on his wife and soon she was afraid to oppose him even in her mind. When the children grew up, he began destroying them, one after the other.

How do you destroy a child?

It's hard to explain, but apparently he accomplished this by playing completely opposite roles at different times. Sometimes, he was kind and loving while other times he was cold and distant. The children never knew what to expect. He would manipulate matters such that all the children would be furious with at least one of their siblings — carefully selecting a different child to be the "perpetrator" each time. In this way, he forced the children to mistrust each other and become utterly dependent upon him.

When the children matured, the real trouble began. He created such havoc that one by one, they began leaving home.

The professionals who stepped in to help the older children thought it was the children who were problematic, but eventually it became clear that the father had a personality disorder that was causing him to undermine his children's emotional stability. They placed a closer watch on the home and removed each child as it became necessary. Not surprisingly, the children *wanted* to leave home. The authorities placed them in safe homes and then did their best to keep the children's whereabouts a secret from their father. In the few cases when the father succeeded in locating the child, he began a campaign of vengeance against the family who had taken him in, until they were sorry they had done so.

The bride's embracement of traditional Judaism helped her deal with the difficulties of her life and focus on her emotional recuperation. Eventually, she was ready to find a suitable spouse and begin building a home of her own.

The family of the groom, who was also a *ba'al teshuvah*, accepted her as a daughter. Their son's happiness was more important to them than their own aspirations, and they went out of their way to accommodate the young couple. The bride's father, sadly, is unable to comprehend another person's happiness.

The Bodyguard

I thought a lot about the bride's father: he was smart and persuasive. He could have been a wonderful father, yet he was a lonely, bitter man whose children wanted nothing to do with him.

Are there others like him who are still devastating the lives of those close to them?

When I think about how he succeeded, within just a few minutes, in convincing me to side with him and very nearly cause serious harm to the people who had hired me, I understand just how difficult it must be to deal with a person like that on a regular basis.

Kindness over Cruelty

> *Two religious children from a dysfunctional home are sent to a secular kibbutz for adoption.*
> *One of them is taken in by a generous, kindhearted man who respects the boy's right to observe the mitzvos.*
> *The other is adopted by a heartless farmer who abuses him cruelly and tries with all his might to force him to abandon religion.*
> *Guess which one of them remained religious?*

I've wanted to write to you for some time now, Rabbi Walder, to tell you my story.

My family moved to Eretz Yisrael approximately forty years ago from a poor country. Although we were very poor, we were staunchly religious.

Our parents had suffered greatly throughout their lives and their health was failing. It wasn't long before our family simply collapsed.

Our parents simply gave up trying to make a go of it. They

stopped working, stopped getting out of bed in the morning, stopped talking. We children were helpless. There was no one to feed us, to cook for us, to dress us or purchase basic necessities.

I don't know how we survived those years. The other families living in our neighborhood were totally normal: The parents woke up every morning and sent their children off to school with a tasty sandwich. They hugged them and said goodbye when they left and greeted them warmly when they returned. They ate lunch and supper; they cleaned the house and did laundry; they went on trips to the park. They talked and sang together on Shabbos.

We had none of that. We simply did what we had to in order to survive. We purchased food and went to school with margarine-smeared bread we'd prepared ourselves. On rare occasions our mother cooked a pot of soup for lunch, but for the most part, we ate hardboiled eggs. No one spoke to us. Our parents were sick and unable to care for us. They never hurt us, but they lacked the strength to provide us with even the barest minimum of a child's needs.

It wasn't long before Social Services stepped in, and the members of our family were dispersed in different directions. We were put up for adoption.

At that time, adoption agencies in Israel worked unhindered. Someone made a decision, someone else signed a paper — and that was it. Families had virtually no chance of overturning a decision — certainly not parents like mine, who were in such bad shape.

My brother Dovid and I were not separated. We were adopted together by a kibbutznik from a settlement up in the north of the country.

To this day, I cannot understand how we were sent to a home like that: two religious children who prayed three times a day to a home where Shabbos and even Yom Kippur were brazenly profaned.

When we arrived at our new home, Motke, the kibbutznik who'd adopted us, began trying to persuade us to remove our yarmulkes. He taunted us mercilessly and horrified us by cursing everything we held dear. At night, my brother would hold me and tell me not to listen to Motke. He said we should insist on wearing our yarmulkes and *tzitzis* and continue praying.

And we did. Motke soon learned that not only was he having no success in persuading us to abandon religion, we were actually becoming stronger in our religious observance.

At first, the other children on the kibbutz fought with us and taunted us relentlessly, but Dovid and I maintained a strong front and refused to be intimidated. After a while, everyone became accustomed to the two boys who wore yarmulkes and observed Shabbos and they accepted us as we were.

Motke, though, considered it a personal affront that we walked around the kibbutz dressed in our religious garb, observing Shabbos and taking care to eat only kosher food. He couldn't bear to see it himself and he was ashamed in front of his friends, as well. I'm not sure he actually received flack from anyone because of the situation, but he sensed that they disapproved, and he took his anger and frustration out on us. When his store of hurtful words and insults was finally depleted, with no change in us at all, he decided he'd had enough.

☙ ☙ ☙

He began abusing us terribly. This man, who presented himself to his fellow kibbutzniks as an enlightened, wonderful individual who had adopted two children, made our lives miserable. He no longer made do with verbal abuse from morning to night; he became physically violent as well.

Since Motke saw my older brother Dovid as the real culprit (rightfully so) in our steadfast resolve to remain religious, it was he who bore the full brunt of Motke's abuse.

My brother was beaten terribly. He was humiliated and demeaned, but the more he suffered, the more stubborn he became. He would tell me stories about Torah giants who sacrificed their lives *al Kiddush Hashem*, and we promised one another that we'd remain loyal to the Torah all our lives, no matter what.

Three years passed and still Motke did not stop trying. At this point, everyone knew he hated us and he worked us to the bone. We were no longer adopted children; we were now his slaves, receiving insults and slaps in exchange for our hard work. I don't know where Social Services had disappeared to. Apparently, they were still wherever they had been when they sent us someplace so different from the home where we'd grown up. They simply didn't think of our welfare.

One day, we were out harvesting olives. At some point, my brother stumbled and fell from exhaustion. Motke became infuriated and began hitting him mercilessly. He got so carried away that he failed to notice a different kibbutznik, Aharon, standing just a few feet away.

Aharon could not believe what he was seeing. "What are you doing, Motke?" he cried out in protest just as Motke delivered another blow to my brother's back.

Motke spun around in alarm and saw Aharon.

"Are you crazy? Why are you hitting him like that?" Aharon demanded.

"Listen, I don't interfere in your life, and you shouldn't interfere in mine," Motke replied, his hands dropping to his sides.

Aharon ignored him. He simply picked up my brother, placed him on his tractor and drove away. He took him to the infirmary, to have him checked by the doctor. Aharon then brought Dovid to his house and began questioning him.

Horrified by what he heard, he decided he could not remain silent. He called a meeting with the heads of the kibbutz to discuss what he had learned.

In those days, kibbutzim were like separate planets. No one dreamed of involving the police. They met a few times in Motke's presence and another few times without him, and finally they reached the decision that my brother should be quietly moved out of Motke's house without involving the authorities.

Aharon, who felt very protective of my brother after hearing what he'd been through, agreed to adopt him in Motke's place. He asked to have me transferred to his care as well, but Motke objected fiercely and threatened to make trouble over Dovid's transfer if they didn't let me stay with him. Motke had connections in Social Services, and the kibbutzniks were well-aware that Motke wouldn't have any problem convincing the authorities that the claims that he abused the children were fabricated.

In addition, Motke threatened his fellow kibbutzniks that he would report certain kibbutz secrets involving egg and milk quotas to the authorities. They preferred to minimize the damage and transfer only my brother to Aharon's care, knowing that Motke abused me to a lesser degree.

Motke told the others that one of the reasons he was

Kindness over Cruelty

allowing them to take my brother was that it was Dovid who was instigating me to remain religious. He was sure that the moment I was free of my brother's influence, I'd quickly abandon my religious fanaticism.

No one objected to what he said. Although some of these people were good and some were less so, the common denominator was that they were all atheists and completely detached from religion. Some even hated religion from an ideological point of view. It was a thorn in everyone's side that two mitzvah-observant children lived among them.

My brother went to live at Aharon's house while I remained with Motke.

If Motke thought that now he'd have an easy time knocking the yarmulke off my head and eradicating the faith in my heart, he was dead wrong. My stubbornness increased tenfold — both because of my talks with my brother and also because of my loyalty to him. I wanted to prove to both him and myself that our separation hadn't changed a thing, and that I was continuing to be a truly Jewish child who was loyal to Hashem and His Torah.

At first, Motke was careful not to hurt me, but his goodwill dissipated quickly, though he was careful not to hit me. He'd suffered embarrassment as a result of the story with my brother, and he feared I might tell Dovid that he was mistreating me — then Aharon would find out and make a huge fuss. So he refrained from physical violence, but he stepped up his verbal abuse and treated me horribly.

Although I was truly happy for my brother, who was enjoying his new life at Aharon's house, deep down I was sorely jealous. Aharon was a wonderful person. He never said a word about my brother's yarmulke or laughed at his prayer habits. He was warm and loving and treated him fairly. He never so much as intimated that my brother's religiousness irked him. I used to tell my brother how hard life was for me, and he continued encouraging me to remain strong, adding that he didn't understand why Motke couldn't be like Aharon, who accepted him for who he was.

Two years passed in this manner. Then my brother completed elementary school and went on to high school, which was located in a different settlement, and we no longer saw each other every day.

One Friday night, I was walking along one of the paths of the kibbutz when I suddenly met my brother.

"Good Shabbos," I greeted him, and he replied with a "good Shabbos" of his own.

I noticed that Dovid wasn't wearing his yarmulke. "You dropped your yarmulke," I pointed out.

"Oh," he replied in confused embarrassment." He stuck his hand in his pocket, withdrew his yarmulke and placed it on his head.

It seemed strange to me, but I said nothing.

A few weeks later, on Shabbos, I passed the area where the boys his age used to sit and sing late into the night. I saw everyone smoking, which was not unusual, but then I saw something that made me freeze in my tracks.

My brother was holding a cigarette.

I ran home and cried all night. The following day, I approached him and said, "What happened, Dovid?"

"Nothing happened," he replied.

I began to cry. "You spoke to me so much about Shabbos, and yesterday... I saw... I saw you holding... a cigarette. Shabbos, Dovid, Sh-a-bbos."

Dovid was shocked. He didn't know what to do with himself. Finally, he decided that the best way to handle the situation was with anger. "What are you, spying on me? I took a cigarette that my friend offered me. I didn't feel comfortable refusing him."

"How come you were perfectly comfortable refusing Motke?" I asked.

He thought for a moment and said, "You know what? You're right. Motke approached it the hard way, and I responded in kind. Now, no one is trying to force me into anything. I don't feel threatened, so... I don't know. Sometimes I lapse."

Suddenly, he opened up and told me that something was happening to him. He still believed in Hashem and His Torah, but he couldn't fight his temptation to do as the others did on Shabbos, and he hadn't donned his *tefillin* for ages.

I was horrified. "What happened, Dovid?" I wept. "How could it be? You were the one who strengthened me against Motke. You made me swear I'd always be observant. How can this be happening?"

Dovid embraced me. "I don't know," he said. "Nothing definite has happened yet, but it's going to. I feel my *yetzer hara* working on me, and I'm not strong enough to fight it off."

We spoke for hours, and we decided that come what may, we wouldn't allow anything to come between us. I returned home and wept bitterly. I knew I wouldn't be able to bear what was going to happen. I didn't say so to Dovid, but I felt he'd betrayed me. Even worse, he'd betrayed his Creator. He had indeed strengthened me against Motke, but then he'd abandoned me for Aharon, and now he was abandoning the Torah as well.

I knew I wouldn't be able to go on like this. Either I'd fall into a depression or I'd follow in Dovid's footsteps.

I didn't know what to do.

I tried to think whom I might turn to for help. Motke was obviously not an option. I thought of Aharon, but immediately realized that he wouldn't help. Aharon had succeeded where Motke had failed. I was too young to understand exactly how it had happened, but I was mature enough to know that my instincts were correct.

The only person I could think of who might be able to help me was "Levi the *Dati*," the fellow who prepared boys on the kibbutz for their bar mitzvah. I approached him and told him about my situation. He told me that he wasn't sure what to do and that he was afraid to advise me to do something that would prove harmful to both me and him (I think he meant that if he were to speak with me about religious matters, he'd lose his livelihood), but he promised to look into it for me.

After pestering him for a week, he gave me the phone number of someone in Bnei Brak.

I called from a public phone. The man who answered introduced himself as a rabbi and sounded very pleasant. I told him, in a nutshell, what I was going through. He suggested that we meet the following week at a shul in a nearby kibbutz.

We met, and I told him my life story. He listened attentively and answered my questions.

Kindness over Cruelty

The questioned that burned in my mind more than any other was how it was possible that my brother, who was free to observe mitzvos, had become irreligious, while I, who suffered greatly for my faith, clung steadfastly to my *Yiddishkeit*.

The *rav* from Bnei Brak told me that in order to answer that question, I had to learn some Jewish history. "Knowing the history of the Jewish People is the key to your question," he said.

He began telling me about the Jewish People, about the persecution they suffered throughout the generations. He spoke about our exile in Egypt and how our ancestors suffered bitterly but refused to change their names, their language, or their mode of dress. He spoke about the Hellenists, who tried to conquer our souls, and about Haman, who tried to exterminate us physically. He told me about the Inquisition and the Marranos, about pogroms and deportations. He said that all these tribulations had not only failed to cause us to abandon Torah and mitzvos; they had only strengthened our faith and resolve.

I listened in fascination. I strongly identified with the Jews throughout the generations who had sacrificed so much *al Kiddush Hashem*. These people had been exiled, tortured, or even killed — but they had perpetuated their Jewish legacy. I wanted to run to Dovid and share my feelings with him, to tell him what he was missing out on. I kept wondering: Why was it that he didn't see what I saw?

As if to answer my question, the *rav* asked me if I was familiar with the word "emancipation."

I had learned the meaning of the word in history class, but I didn't really remember what it meant.

"Napoleon Bonaparte, who ruled France some 200 years

ago, was the first ruler in Europe's blood-soaked, racial history to grant the Jews equal rights to those of all other citizens. Sounds like a wonderful step that should have been good for the Jews, right?"

"Of course," I replied.

"But do you know what it caused?" the *rav* sighed. "Emancipation, equality and enlightenment succeeded in accomplishing what all the decrees, persecution, killing, looting and deportations suffered by the Jewish People did not. Emancipation distanced the Jewish People from the Torah with a friendly smile, encouraging them warmly to embrace false ideologies and stop observing the mitzvos. Many of our people became assimilated among the nations and converted.

I stared at him in shock. "But why? How did it happen?"

"Because the *yetzer hara* has its own technique. As long as the *yetzer tov* is on its guard because the *yetzer hara* is trying to force the person to do wrong — the *yetzer tov* will triumph. But when bad disguises itself as good, speaking softly and warmly embracing, the *yetzer tov* is lulled to sleep, and when a guard falls asleep on the job, the enemy is free to invade and conquer.

"And you know what?" the *rav* added. "It works the other way, too. One can lull the *yetzer hara* to sleep by working with goodness and kindness rather than force and threats. When a person feels hurt and under attack, the *yetzer hara* remains alert and prevents him from doing *teshuvah*, but if he is shown the right way in a kind and loving fashion, the *yetzer hara* goes to sleep and the *yetzer tov* can do its work.

"Do you see?" he explained to me. "You'll never be able to change a person by force, for better or for worse. The only way to change a person is with kindness and pleasantness.

He went on to relate a parable I'll never forget: The sun

Kindness over Cruelty

and the wind once had an argument over who was stronger. They decided to see which of them would be successful in removing a man's coat from his body. The wind whipped mercilessly about, trying to blow the coat off, but the man just wrapped himself in it all the more tightly.

When it was the sun's turn, it simply shone brightly. Soon it was so warm that the man himself took off the coat.

There was no need to explain. I understood perfectly.

◆ ◆ ◆

The *rav* suggested that I wait until my eighteenth birthday before switching from the secular high school I was attending to a yeshivah. He explained that until I reached the age of eighteen, I was not yet permitted to make independent decisions.

In the meantime, I maintained contact with him. We spoke often, and he gave me holy books that bolstered my faith and increased my knowledge of Torah, Jewish thought and *mussar*. When I reached the age of seventeen, I decided to attend yeshivah — and not just any yeshivah: Yeshivas Ponevezh in Bnei Brak.

Of course, this was no simple matter, but my determination, my ability and the *rav*'s assistance helped me get accepted. Motke made some trouble, but by the time he figured out where I was and tried to do something about it, I'd already celebrated my eighteenth birthday and he was powerless to stop me.

I spent six years studying at the yeshivah, and at the age of twenty-four, I married a girl from a *chareidi* family in Yerushalayim. We set up our home in Yerushalayim, where I now work as a *ra"m*. No one knows anything about my past.

The bottom line is that my incredibly difficult childhood

built me up. I perceive things differently than other people do. I am aware of how joyful I ought to be that I merited being one of Hashem's beloved children, studying His Torah and observing His commandments while raising a beautiful family.

Beyond that, I have an important message that I feel an urgent need to transmit to the public at large.

From my vantage point, it is crystal-clear to me that with regard to *chinuch*, it is extremely important to employ "the good approach" in all situations and at all costs.

Ever since my childhood, I've been aware of the power struggle between the *yetzer tov* and the *yetzer hara*, both of which were created by *Hakadosh Baruch Hu* so that we would have free choice.

The trouble is that people tend to think that they're stronger than these inclinations and that they can coerce a person to triumph over his *yetzer hara* (or over his *yetzer tov*, God forbid).

The nations of the world thought that by abusing us, exiling us, and killing us, they'd subjugate our good inclination, but mortal man can never vanquish a human inclination. As soon as war was declared, the *yetzer tov* rose to the challenge and triumphed.

Some people try to use the same tactic on the *yetzer hara*: they hurt and insult the wrongdoer, humiliating him or even beating him in an attempt to crush the *yetzer hara*, but it is precisely under these conditions that the *yetzer hara* rallies and triumphs.

What we must do is employ goodness and kindness in order to give the *yetzer tov* an edge. Instead of trying to conquer the *yetzer hara* by force, we should focus on encouraging and strengthening the *yetzer tov*.

Kindness over Cruelty

From time to time, mostly at family events, I meet my brother. He is completely secular, but he is not anti-religious. He observes Yom Kippur. We are on close terms and we often argue about various issues, though we each know we don't stand a chance of convincing the other.

We are already both of the age where it is perfectly obvious where life has taken us. My brother has two children: one is a bachelor while the other has given him one grandchild. He never sees them because they live abroad. From time to time, they send pictures.

I have nine children, six of whom are married, as well as twenty grandchildren.

Motke and Aharon are no longer alive. I can't say I thank Motke or that Dovid hates Aharon. It doesn't work that way. A person can't love someone who hurt him, nor can he hate one who has been kind to him. I cannot forget what Motke did to me in my childhood, even though I know that his behavior is what protected my adherence to Judaism. Dovid loves and respects Aharon even though he is aware that his love is what distanced him from his roots, albeit unintentionally.

※ ※ ※

We have a longstanding agreement that I'd like to share with you and your readers: that the only way to influence others is with kindness and goodness, and a sure way to get others to do the opposite of what you want is to be tough and mean to him.

Motke attempted to uproot us from our religion with cruelty — and failed dismally. Aharon went the kind route, caressing Dovid like the sun — and succeeded where Motke had failed.

The lesson to be learned here is somewhat ironic. The

opposition of those who are against us only serves to strengthen us in remaining steadfast in our Torah observance. Were they to embrace us, the danger to our existence would be very real. Just like Motke's attempts at coercion, their hatred causes us to cling to our values even more tightly.

An even more important insight can be gleaned by parents whose children are somewhat lax in their observance of mitzvos or slack with regard to *davening* or Torah study. Don't use force. If you ever find yourself trying to force your child to do something by screaming or hitting, God forbid, think of Motke and restrain yourself. Then think of Aharon and how successful he was at influencing Dovid — albeit in an undesirable direction — and learn from him how to draw children closer to Hashem and His Torah.

On Pesach, when everyone asks why we recite a blessing on the *maror* — it's so bitter, after all — I smile and recite the blessing with great fervor. It was the *maror* that Motke fed me that saved me; it helped me to remain a Torah-true Jew.

8

The Chef

A talented and capable young man experiences frustration when he cannot find his place among his peers.

On a weekend getaway arranged by his yeshivah, trouble arises when a very crucial person — the cook — fails to show up.

When the heads of the yeshivah inform the boys that they have no choice but to send them home, the hero of our story offers to take the cook's place.

This opportunity can lead to either disaster or growth, because a person must "eat" whatever he "cooks" up for himself...

I'm thirty-one years old, married, and the father of several adorable children.

I'd like to begin my story from the middle.

At the age of sixteen, I was a very quiet, withdrawn young man. I was terribly lonely. True, I was surrounded by other boys my age all day and I'd never been in an argument with any of them — but I'd never developed a friendship with any of them, either. This situation was a natural continuation of my childhood years.

I had been quiet as a child and I continued to be withdrawn as a *bachur*. The odds were that I'd continue to be shy and timid as an adult as well.

I think that only someone who's been there can truly understand what it feels like to be a quiet, timid student among outgoing peers.

If I had to come up with a comparison, I'd choose that of a deaf man at a wedding. He sees everyone dancing, swaying and singing; he is there among them — but he's not a part of it.

Or maybe a more apt comparison is that of a person standing outside a house in which there is a party taking place. He hears the sound of laughter, but not only doesn't it make him happy, it actually saddens him, because he feels left out.

In your book *Kidspeak 6*, you write about a child who is very quiet "on the outside," but is brimming with great ideas and the desire to implement them, only he can't bring himself to speak up. When I read that, I felt that you were describing me.

The reason I was so withdrawn was a direct result of the hardships I had endured as a child, but as I said before, I've started my story from the middle, and I'll return to the beginning at a later point.

It seemed to me that nothing would ever change in my life. I was a social outcast. There was nothing I excelled at, and to most of my peers, I might as well have been air.

And then came the yeshivah weekend getaway.

I was in tenth grade. My yeshivah, like many others, had arranged a *bein hazemanim* weekend getaway. As an aside, I

The Chef

would like to say that this is a great idea for keeping boys off the streets during the summer. Nowadays, the street is a terrible place, and a full month without a proper framework can wreak great havoc with *bachurim.*

The getaway was held at a site with a number of bungalows, a dining hall, and lovely grounds. We arrived there on Thursday, shortly before noon. The rooms were quite comfortable and the view was just lovely. Only one thing was missing.

A cook.

The yeshivah had hired a cook to prepare our meals. The yeshivah had purchased the necessary supplies, but the cook was a no-show.

They called him and he said he had a problem and wouldn't be able to come until Friday.

There was no choice. A few *bachurim* prepared scrambled eggs, and they *looked* like they had been prepared by a couple of *bachurim.*

Although they didn't look very appetizing, the scrambled eggs actually tasted reasonably decent. That's how we survived until Friday.

Friday arrived, and everyone assumed the cook was hard at work cooking our Shabbos meals. Suddenly, someone remembered to check whether he had indeed arrived.

He had not.

It was 11:00 A.M. Shabbos would be coming in at 7:00 P.M.

The staff began making phone calls, and when they finally reached the cook, this was his reply: "I can't make it. I'm not coming."

"Why didn't you let us know?"

"I figured you'd realize on your own and work something out," he said.

If his lack of responsibility was any indication of the way he cooked, chances are we'd all have died of food poisoning.

The staff tried calling a few different people to find a substitute cook, but by noon it was clear to everyone that although we had lots of chicken, meat, fish, vegetables, spices and the ingredients for side dishes and desserts — there was no one to cook them.

The staff was under enormous pressure. After discussing the situation among themselves, they assembled us in the dining room and said, "We've reached the conclusion that Shabbos without food is not Shabbos. We have no choice but to arrange for the buses to take you back home. Please let your parents know to expect you so they can make the necessary arrangements."

Turmoil ensued. Many *bachurim* said their parents had gone on vacation and they had nowhere to go. Some of these *bachurim* made arrangements to go to a friend's house, but others still had nowhere to go.

Once again, the staff discussed the situation. They were at a loss for what to do. "Does anyone have a suggestion?" the *mashgiach* asked us boys.

There was a tense silence and then — to this day, I don't know where I found the courage — I said, "I think I can cook the food for Shabbos."

"What?!"

Everyone looked at me in total disbelief. "You can cook the food for Shabbos?" the *mashgiach* repeated back, his tone of voice making his skepticism perfectly clear.

"Yes," I said. "I can."

"But how... Did you take cooking lessons?"

The Chef

"No, but… I think I can do it."

"Do you know how to cook, or do you *think* you know how to cook?" asked a *bachur* from the eleventh grade. "You see, we already had a cook who *thought* he would come here."

We all laughed.

"I know how to cook," I said, my self-confidence alarming even me. They looked at me, and something about my confident demeanor persuaded them that I was speaking the truth.

"Okay," said the *mashgiach*. "What do you need?"

"I need five *bachurim* to help me."

"What kind of help?"

"Peeling vegetables and all kinds of other stuff. I'll show them what to do."

"Do we have any volunteers?" the *mashgiach* asked.

Five boys volunteered — three from the eleventh grade and two from my own grade.

"Go with him," the *mashgiach* said.

I received the keys to the kitchen and the walk-in refrigerator and freezer, and the group of five followed me.

I entered the walk-in refrigerator and instructed the boys to carry all the vegetables out and place them on the counter near the sink. There was also several boxes of filleted fish which would make a tasty appetizer.

Then I went into the freezer and, with the help of three *bachurim*, lugged out the boxes of chickens. I opened the warm water and defrosted the chickens.

I then turned to face my crew. "Okay, now we peel the vegetables," I said.

We had no working peelers, so we used knives. It took the five of us about half an hour, during which time we chatted about the weekend and the programs and activities we'd enjoyed thus far. For the first time in my life, I was carrying on an easy-flowing conversation with my classmates.

We finished peeling and I divided the boys into groups.

I asked two of them to chop the vegetables for the soup, demonstrating on a squash, an onion, a carrot and a potato.

I instructed two other boys to prepare a salad, showing them how to chop the vegetables fine.

I asked the fifth boy to check rice (for a side dish) and beans for the *cholent*, demonstrating how to do the job properly.

In the meantime, I poured some oil into two large pans and began frying onions.

The kitchen was a hubbub of activity as I moved between the fish, the soup and the *cholent*, issuing instructions, tasting and adjusting the seasoning. The boys were amazed. They kept showering me with compliments and asking, "How do you know all this?"

I set another pot on the fire and sent one of my workers to request permission to purchase more supplies. When permission was granted, I sent a *bachur* from my grade to buy a few packages of bittersweet chocolate and pareve whipped topping. In the meantime, I beat eggs and added the beans and barley to the *cholent*.

The yeshivah staff came to the kitchen for an official visit. We had no time to pay any attention to them. They simply stood on the side in wide-eyed silence, watching us operate as a team as I ran the show with supreme self-confidence. Today, years later, I understand what a huge surprise it must have been for them to see me — a quiet, timid *bachur* who almost never opened his mouth — functioning like a born leader.

The Chef

An hour later, everything was bubbling merrily on the stove. I took another pot and asked my crew to fill it with eggs. "This is for the eggs and onions for the Shabbos day *seudah*," I explained to the *bachur* who set the pot on the stove. While the eggs were cooking, I prepared delicious chopped liver and stored it in the refrigerator.

At five o'clock, I turned my attention to setting the tables.

I asked two additional boys to help me. We spread tablecloths on the tables, and then we put a plate, silverware and a cup by each place setting. I showed them how to put a napkin decoratively in each cup. They couldn't believe how simple and easy it was.

Then we returned to the kitchen to plate the fish. I showed my "staff" how to drizzle some garlic sauce on each plate, then lay the fish on top alongside some vegetables and a slice of lemon, and then drizzle some more garlic sauce on top. The boys followed my instructions and the results were stunning. It looked like a unique gourmet dish.

Next, we transferred the salads into pretty bowls. The chicken and soup were ready by now, so I prepared to make dessert.

I prepared individual mini chocolate cakes with "molten" centers. The *bachurim* helping me kept sticking their fingers in the batter and licking them, until I yelled at them to stop.

"The yeshivah is in for a real surprise," they kept saying. "No one dreams we're going to have food like this." We decided not to let anyone into the kitchen so the menu would be a surprise.

Being partners in a secret with other boys my age was a heady experience.

Half an hour before Shabbos, everything was ready. I went to see how my recruits were managing with the tables.

They couldn't stop staring at me in surprise as I straightened a napkin here and a plate there.

Shabbos arrived. We *davened Minchah, kabbalas Shabbos* and *Ma'ariv* — and then everyone entered the dining room.

From that moment on, I was the recipient of more compliments than I'd received in my entire life up to then.

First of all, everyone was amazed at how appealing the tables looked. They gushed over the napkins and the salads (which were store-bought, but when you take them out of their containers and place them in attractive dishes, they somehow look far more appetizing).

And then the fish was served.

I can't begin to describe what went on when the boys saw the beautifully arranged plates. At first, they weren't sure how to handle such gourmet fare. Then they tasted it and everyone in turn came to tell me how delicious it was. Many boys asked for seconds.

The fish was followed by a *dvar Torah* and *zemiros*, and then we served the soup. I know this may sound repetitive, but the soup was absolutely delicious.

In the kitchen, one of the eleventh-grade *bachurim* said to me conspiratorially, "Wait until we serve dessert. The guys won't believe their eyes!"

His eyes were filled with admiration. I'd never been the object of admiring glances before. Come to think of it, I'd never been the object of *any* glances before.

The dessert was indeed so delicious and beautiful that I simply couldn't handle the rush of compliments.

The *rosh yeshivah* rose to speak. He based his talk on the idea that one should never despair; that even the most

The Chef

hopeless situation can be turned around. Of course, he brought the most current example to prove his point, describing how the staff had been about to give up when suddenly I came along and saved the day. He praised me excessively, saying "Where were you until now?" and bemoaning the fact that because I was so modest and refined, no one had ever realized what unique capabilities I had. I must admit that I lapped up the praise and the applause. I received in a few hours what my peers had received in more modest amounts over the course of their lives.

After the *seudah*, the *bachurim* retired to their rooms. Many boys sought me out and wanted to speak with me, but I was busy assembling my crew in the kitchen to discuss the following day's *seudah*. At this point, we were a team, united by our common goal of serving delicious and beautiful Shabbos fare.

The following day was a repeat of the Friday night *seudah*. The chopped liver was so delicious that even the pickiest eaters showered me with compliments. I won't even begin to describe the response when we served dessert.

For *seudah shlishis*, we served dairy foods.

I set out a smorgasbord of cheeses: some flavored with garlic, some with dill, and some with scallions. There were also yellow cheeses, smoked fish, quiches I'd prepared and, of course, whatever was left of the salads. It looked lovely, even though the various cheeses were really the same basic cheese with different seasonings added.

Then the *mashgiach* asked me to speak.

I refused. I'd never spoken in pubic before and I wasn't about to start then.

"I'm not asking you to speak *divrei Torah*," he said. "Just tell us how you learned to cook so well."

I sat in my place, somewhat uncomfortable with one hundred and twenty pairs of eyes trained on me.

I knew that my peers had no idea what stood behind it all.

I vacillated for a moment and then — I don't know where I found the courage — I decided to tell my story.

I wrote in the beginning of my letter that I had decided to begin in the middle. Now for the beginning.

✎ ✎ ✎

"When I was eleven years old," I began, "my mother became ill with a terminal disease."

Utter silence reigned.

"We watched her deteriorate slowly. At first, she was merely very weak, but then she began radiation and chemotherapy treatment, and she literally could not move. For many long weeks, she wasn't home at all.

"We were six children. I was the oldest. Suddenly, my shirts weren't laundered and we had to eat cheese sandwiches for breakfast, lunch and supper. Sometimes we had scrambled eggs.

"One day, one of my aunts came to cook for us. She prepared a meal like we hadn't eaten in weeks. I asked my aunt to please teach me how to cook, and she did. I learned to prepare salads, omelets, soup and even chicken. Later, she taught me to make potato *kugel* and *cholent*. My mother would come home from time to time and I would prepare delicious meals in her honor. Most of the time she was too weak to speak, but her eyes told me she was pleased and oh so proud of me."

It was hard for me to speak at this point, but I pushed myself to go on.

"Eventually, I felt confident enough to experiment on my

The Chef

own. I learned which seasonings went well with what, and I developed some new recipes. As far as meals were concerned, our home was functioning normally once again. At least the children had hot, nutritious, homemade meals."

I paused, overcome with emotion, as I recalled that difficult period in my life. Although I kept my tears in check, I saw that many *bachurim* and staff members were crying. Some of them were hiding their faces in their hands while others allowed their tears to flow freely.

I went on with my tale, pausing now and again when necessary to regain my composure. Every time I stopped, I heard the sound of quiet sobbing.

"And then my mother passed away. In a letter she left behind, she praised me for taking her place and asked me to continue so that the children would have proper meals even after she was gone.

"We sat *shivah*. When it was over, I continued cooking for everyone until my father remarried a year later. Our new mother was a great cook, so there was no longer any need for me to do the cooking. I still enjoy cooking, though, and every so often, when I return home, I join my stepmother in the kitchen. We exchange ideas for all kinds of dishes and flavorings. This helped cement my bond with her, and the other children followed my lead in accepting her, so that the transition was relatively smooth."

When I finished speaking, the *mashgiach* rose and embraced me. Then all the staff members, whose faces were still red from crying, followed suit. The *bachurim* all shook my hands, their eyes filled with respect and admiration. Then we sat down and we began singing slow songs filled with longing, until well after Shabbos ended.

That Shabbos changed my life. I no longer had a problem interacting with other boys. I didn't turn into a boisterous extrovert overnight, but I found it much easier to express myself. I was no longer relegated to the sidelines.

I went on to *yeshivah gedolah* and married soon after. I have four wonderful children and *baruch Hashem*, I have a position in *chinuch* at which I'm doing very well.

Cooking is still a hobby for me. Why shouldn't my wife and children benefit from my knowledge? At special occasions, I always treat them to at least one tasty dish.

I don't do it only for them; I do it at least as much for myself. Cooking, like drawing or writing, is an art. I have a special connection to this art — it is especially close to my heart because it gave me the chance to become a part of society, to express myself and be successful. It turned my entire life around.

Rabbi Walder, I know that you recommend that children find a hobby where they can shine, such as carpentry, art or writing. Allow me to suggest another option: Cooking!

9

A Simple Jew

A family of new olim from the United States tries to adjust to life in Israel.

For some reason, they can't seem to integrate into the Ashkenazic community despite the fact that they are Ashkenazim. On the other hand, they receive lots of warmth from the Sephardic community.

They decide to become Sephardim, but fail to anticipate the implications of such a step.

My story is rather strange and unusual.

I recently read a story in one of your books, a story about Ashkenazic discrimination and the terrible injustice to high school girls and yeshivah boys. I decided to write you my personal story, which presents the problem in an altogether different light.

I attended a Sephardic Talmud Torah, and my peers there treated me horribly throughout the years.

If you're not quite sure why, perhaps the following line will explain.

My family is of Ashkenazic origin. I have blond hair and blue eyes and a decidedly Ashkenazic name. Now you must be wondering what I was doing in a Sephardic yeshivah.

You see, my parents are American *ba'alei teshuvah*. Before they became religious, my father was a guitarist in a rock group, and my mother was their drummer. I'm sure you're beginning to get the picture.

My parents traveled a long and winding road, including a trip to India, before they finally arrived at the absolute truth and returned to Judaism.

They moved to Israel, but they weren't received very well. They couldn't find their place. My father attended an Ashkenazic shul for a year, and not once did anyone approach him to inquire what his name was or whether he needed anything. Everyone just assumed he was a tourist who was in the country for a short while and would soon return home. The fact that this "short while" lasted a year never inspired anyone to rethink his calculation.

Then he went to a Sephardic synagogue, and he was immediately greeted with great warmth. He was given an *aliyah* and someone invited him to his son's *bar mitzvah* even though he'd never met him before. That was a smorgasbord of an affair that only Sephardim know how to put on.

My father took the invitation seriously and even brought along his wife and children. Astoundingly, everyone greeted him as if it was the most natural thing in the world. They also asked him to play something on an electric guitar, and that was the first time I saw my father play. I only thank God that my mother didn't offer to play the drums...

The result of all this was that my parents decided they no longer wanted to be Ashkenazim.

And so, with no advance warning and no official ceremony, we suddenly became Sephardim.

When I say we became Sephardim, I mean lock, stock and barrel: We began attending a Sephardic synagogue, switched to the Sephardic *nusach* of *davening*, and adopted Sephardic customs such as eating legumes on Pesach. For people like my parents, who had gone from being hippies to Buddhists to *chareidim*, switching gears midway and becoming Sephardim presented no problem at all.

Since we were now full-fledged Sephardim, I had to switch to a Sephardic Talmud Torah.

I later learned that the principal had tried to talk my father out of the idea, but he had refused to listen. Instead, he had shown signs of hurt that they didn't want to accept me. In the end, the principal agreed to accept me, though he warned my father to expect some trouble.

At that point, I knew nothing about the tensions between Ashkenazim and Sephardim. I think that the first time I understood that there was some sort of problem was in the second grade, when one of the kids began calling me "*vuzvuz*." Of course, all the other kids immediately followed suit. I asked my father what the word meant, but he had no idea. I asked the children what it meant, and they explained that I was an "Ashkentuzi." I denied the allegations hotly, although I had no idea what they meant.

My friends tried to convince me that I really was an Ashkenazi. I asked my father whether it was true, and he said, "Not exactly. We used to be Ashkenazim, but not anymore."

I returned to class brimming with self-confidence and explained that although my family used to be Ashkenazim, we were now Sephardim. It actually helped. The children accepted my explanation for the time being. But it didn't last long.

In the sixth grade, it began all over again. I think it happened as a result of the political crisis between the Yahadus

HaTorah and Shas parties. One day, a kid shouted, "You Ashkenazi, you! Get out of here!" From that moment on, I was subjected to a barrage of insults and harassment.

The kids taunted and humiliated me, calling me "white," "Ashkenazi (pronouncing the end of the word like Nazi)" and "*vuzvuz*." It didn't stop at words, either; I was regularly beaten. At first, I told my father about what was happening, and he tried to do something about the situation, but nothing helped. At some point, I just stopped telling him about it. I understood that he was unable to help me, no matter how badly he wanted to. I simply suffered in silence. I was a social outcast.

In the seventh grade, I had a wonderful teacher who immediately understood what was going on, and at some point early in the school year, he announced that anyone who hurt me in any way would find himself outside the Talmud Torah.

A few kids tested him and he suspended them without even listening to their side of the story. When they returned, neither they nor any of the other children dared lift a finger against me, but the taunts continued, and they were no less painful than the physical kicks and jabs had been. When the teacher put an end to those as well, they were replaced by a quiet, sullen hatred on the part of my peers.

I cannot begin to explain how much I suffered. It was absolutely unbearable.

The teacher, whom I will always remember for the humanity and warmth he showed me, spoke with me about the situation, and I told him that nothing could be done. True, no one dared hit me or call me names anymore, but it was impossible to eradicate the hatred in the boys' hearts. He told

A Simple Jew

me that he would speak with my parents and he followed up by asking them to come see him at his house.

After the meeting, my father asked to speak with me. He seemed very pained and concerned as he told me that he'd had no idea I was suffering so badly. He told me that after discussing the situation with my teacher, they had arrived at the conclusion that there was no choice but to send me to an Ashkenazic Talmud Torah.

I was stunned. Was that what my teacher had said?

"Yes, he loves you and cares about you."

"He loves me? Is that why he's sending me to the Ashkentuzim?"

"What?" My father was shocked. "What did you say?"

"I refuse to learn with Ashkenazim. I hate them. They make me sick."

I could tell my father was utterly shocked. He spoke to my mother and they both asked me, "Did the Ashkenazim ever do anything to harm you?"

"No, but... they're Ashkenazim."

Astonishingly enough, the abuse I had suffered had created an inexplicable hatred toward my natural ethnic extraction.

Today, as an adult, I can understand how this happened. I recall reading a story entitled *The Teacher's Son* in one of your books. The story described the subconscious hatred a child felt toward his father, who had been his teacher, as a result of the abuse he had suffered at the hands of his peers because of the situation. I identified very strongly with the theory that the psyche hates that which causes him harm. I hated Ashkenazim. I perceived them to be the root cause of my pain.

My parents took me for therapy, and the therapist reached the conclusion that my parents had to be very clear on whether they were Ashkenazim or Sephardim, because I and the rest of my siblings were being torn and were liable to pay a heavy emotional price.

My parents were very torn. On the one hand, they had already set down roots in the Sephardic community, but on the other, their children were white as snow and looked unmistakably Ashkenazi, and they studied in a framework where the topic of ethnicity was relevant on a daily basis.

They decided to take an incredible step. One day, they returned to their birthplace, the United States of America.

All of a sudden, it made no difference whether we were Ashkenazim or Sephardim. My father continued *davening* in a Sephardic synagogue. We attended community schools and I never heard a discussion or debate concerning the Sephardi–Ashkenazi topic again.

We healed completely.

I'm sure there will be some who will say that we paid a price for this "recuperation." After all, we left the community in Eretz Yisrael, which is stronger than the one we came to in America. On the other hand, we never really belonged to Israeli society, because it never truly recognized or accepted us. Perhaps the Sephardic community wanted to accept us, but it was unsuccessful.

I think my story can describe the pain of thousands of Sephardic boys, girls and teens who study in Ashkenazic yeshivos or seminaries in the Israeli *chareidi* community.

Many of them experience the same type of suffering I did in my childhood, be it name-calling or some other type of hostile behavior. I'm not blaming anyone. I know that the Lithuanian Ashkenazic community has done much to

A Simple Jew

welcome Sephardim into their ranks, but as long as the current walls between Sephardim and Ashkenazim remain intact, people will continue to hurt and be hurt by one another.

Generations of people will be badly hurt and most Ashkenazim, who have never experienced this type of pain, will never be able to truly understand its depth.

Except for me, of course.

I have a feeling that Hashem sent me, a lone Ashkenazi, into Sephardic society so that I would experience the pain and then tell my Ashkenazi brethren what it's like.

You ask who I am today?

I'm neither an Ashkenazi nor a Sephardi. I'm just a simple Jew.

The Dirty Side of Cleanliness

Which is worse: A dirty, neglected household where no one cleans a thing for months on end, or a tip-top household where every speck of dust is reason for screaming, insults and hysteria?

The following story might shed some light on the answer, in addition to providing a reminder that both extremes are unacceptable.

In one of the *People Speak* books, you published the story of a social worker who entered a terribly disorderly and filthy house, cleaned it up, and rehabilitated the family who lived there.

When I was a girl, there was a family like that who lived in my building, and I saw up close everything that you described in your book.

I was nine years old at the time, but smart enough to understand that something wasn't right with that family: the mess was indescribable and every item they owned was terribly neglected.

The Dirty Side of Cleanliness

I remember clearly the day that house was cleared of junk that had been piling up inside for ages. They went to great lengths to place the bags far from our building so that the neighbors wouldn't make the connection between the filth and the place it had originated from, but we would have known the truth even if they had tossed the trash in a different country. We'd been living with this family and their filth for years, even if we'd never actually seen it. They locked that house like a fortress, but the stench couldn't be contained or concealed, and we suffered from the insects that were constantly drawn to their home.

Today, I ask myself how we managed to live with these neighbors, even treating them with the same friendliness as the others. I think that we simply differentiated between the terrible problem they had, which apparently stemmed from either an emotional problem or extreme laziness on the part of the parents, and the people, who seemed perfectly ordinary.

You see, there was nothing about these neighbors, neither the parents nor the children, to indicate that anything was amiss. They were dressed normally, although their clothes did look somewhat rumpled. They spoke, played and laughed like everyone else.

One of the girls in that family was my age, and we were good friends. She was definitely not emotionally neglected in any way. Apparently, the neglect was environmental only, not emotional. The parents had a wonderful relationship with their children.

The years passed, and eventually I went to high school with my neighbor, where we each made new friends who had attended other elementary schools.

One of them, Miri (not her real name), was a slight,

delicate, almost fragile girl. She was considered a very good girl, but it was clear she wasn't happy.

She almost never spoke or smiled. Her face was always clouded by an indefinable shadow. We had the impression that she was suffering from depression.

About six months into the school year, Miri became friendly with my neighbor, Dina (not her real name). They soon became very close, though it was obvious that Dina needed additional friends as Miri barely opened her mouth. Dina tried to help Miri integrate with the other girls by pulling her along with her whenever a group of girls was chatting together. This way, at least Miri was able to hear what the girls were discussing.

One day, Dina said to me, "I think Miri has a problem. Maybe we can help her."

We decided to take her to a nearby park and encourage her to open up and tell us what was troubling her.

We went to the park a few times and saw that she was really relaxed in our company. One day, as we were sitting on the grass chatting about nothing in particular, I said to Miri, "Tell me, can you explain why you seem so depressed?"

I asked the question with a half-smile, but I was really very serious.

Miri looked at me sadly but said nothing.

We began pressing her to open up to us. We reminded her that we were her friends and assured her we'd keep her secret. Eventually, she opened up and told us the story of her life.

"My mother," she said, "is an extremely tense woman, especially with regard to cleanliness. She is suspicious and mistrustful even of her children, constantly hovering over us and

The Dirty Side of Cleanliness

criticizing us. She terrorizes us, to the point that we live in fear that nothing should be out of place. *Chas v'shalom* that someone makes a mess, because then she loses control completely. When that happens, everyone walks on eggshells or simply leaves the house."

"What about your father?" I asked.

She sighed. "He's the worst off of us all. He constantly has to maneuver between his concern for us and the need to protect my mother's dignity." Miri explained that her father and the children had developed a method of communicating via meaningful looks. "He might tell us, 'Your behavior is inexcusable!'" Miri said, "but with his eyes, he says, *It's okay. I understand you.*"

When she had finished describing the situation, she burst into inconsolable tears.

We sat there in silence, not knowing what to do.

"You've got to get help," I said. "You can't keep suffering like this."

"Where should we turn?" Miri asked helplessly. "Who do you think can help us?"

"I know who you should turn to," Dina said suddenly.

"Who?" we asked.

"Well, I'll have to disclose a secret of my own," Dina replied, "but I don't mind, because one of you knows the truth in any case." She looked at me. "As for the other... I don't mind if she knows. She looked at Miri. "You told me about your life; now I'll tell you about mine."

For the first time, I heard Dina describe the terrible neglect at her house.

◆ ◆ ◆

She described the terrible clutter in her home and how

the children had suffered because of it. A few times, the children had tried to do something about the situation, but they'd quickly despaired because their parents seemed unable to handle any change from their usual disorderly lifestyle.

Then a social worker showed up and cleaned and organized the house. Dina described how difficult it had been for her mother to accept the social worker's intervention and how the latter had finally convinced her to make some semblance of order in her life.

"My parents showered us with love and warmth," Dina said. "Our suffering was physical in nature rather than emotional. When the social worker came, she solved the problem and today everything's fine. I think I should contact her, and she'll visit your house and find the right way to solve your problem, too. She's very tactful. Maybe she'll be able to ease your mother's terrible tension."

"Don't you dare do anything of the sort," Miri warned.

"Why not?" Dina asked.

"My mother's a psychologist," Miri said quietly. "There's no way she'll allow a social worker to interfere. That would set our house on fire."

We were shocked into silence.

"I can't believe it," Dina murmured after a long moment. "How can it be? I mean, a psychologist is supposed to treat such cases, no?"

Miri began to cry. "My 'outside' mother is all sweetness and light," she said, "but my 'at home' mother makes our life bitter. My mother has a problem and there's no one we can turn to; do you understand? You're suggesting I contact a social worker? My mother's a psychologist, and not just any psychologist, but a very highly respected one. But we suffer from her! Who will heal the doctor?"

The Dirty Side of Cleanliness

It was then that I understood just how complex life can be.

I had always pitied Dina terribly, thinking that her problem was simply awful, but now I realized how wrong I'd been. Dina was a warm, happy, loving girl. Miri, on the other hand, was the daughter of a woman who had a career in helping people with emotional difficulties, and she was a withdrawn, tense, trampled-on young lady. She had no one to help her, and even if she eventually found someone, it might be too late.

I decided to speak with my parents about Miri's situation. A few days later, I approached Miri with a solution.

"You've got to contact Welfare Services and ask for help," I told her. "There must be someone who can rescue you all from the terrible situation in which you find yourselves." I told Miri that while I understood that it would be terribly uncomfortable for her to take such a step, she could rest assured that her secret would be safe, because there was a law requiring people who worked at the welfare office to protect the confidentiality of anyone who asked for help.

It took a while for Miri to be persuaded, but in the end, she did it. She and her family endured a difficult period, but after half a year, she approached the two of us and thanked us.

"My conversation with you was my family's salvation," she said. She didn't offer many details, but she did reveal that her mother was in treatment and that her attitude had changed completely.

"The truth is that as soon as the matter was exposed, eighty percent of our problems were resolved, because my mother was always concerned about what people would think. She's working on the other twenty percent — working hard. Today, she is no longer as furious with me as she was at first."

Apparently, no one can say what "normal" is, and sometimes, excessive obsessing on cleanliness and order can cause greater distress than filth and neglect.

Seeking Atonement

After years of being raised by her mother, a young girl seeks to learn her father's identity.
Her discovery shatters her world, causing her to regret having asked...
As if that weren't enough, her father suddenly reappears in her life, and her entire world caves in...

For some time, I've known my life story would be perfect for your books. It took me awhile to overcome my fear that I'd be recognized, but now I decided I was ready.

My life can be divided into a few parts.

I remember my early childhood years as a time of goodness and abundance. My memories of this time are rather vague, because I was really young, but still, my mind contains images of outings, clothing, gifts, trips abroad and a doting father playing with me. I had an idyllic childhood.

But life as I knew it stopped when I was six.

My parents divorced. I don't remember anything of what

went on, just that we suddenly moved to a small house in a poor neighborhood, and that we exchanged happiness and joy for poverty and sadness.

I remember my mother changing, withdrawing into herself to the point where she found it difficult to care for me.

And my father simply disappeared from my life.

I would ask my mother where my father was, and she'd respond with anger and ask me not to speak of him.

To this day, I don't know how I handled that.

My memories of my father had been only good ones, filled with hugs, sweets and ice cream. But suddenly, he was gone, and I... I accepted it as a fact of life, perhaps because I didn't know then what I know today — that there *are* children who grow up with both a mommy and a daddy who stay with them for always. Perhaps I just assumed that this was the way life was for everyone. Or perhaps I just suppressed my questions.

From that point on, my childhood was far from easy. I was an only child with only my somewhat depressed and often irritable mother for company. To make matters worse, we had no money.

At about the age of twelve or thirteen, I began questioning my mother about my father: who he was and to where he had disappeared. She refused to answer me, and every time I mentioned him, she reacted with terrible anger. "It's none of your business," she would say. "Don't bring up the subject again."

This response quelled my interest for a while, but after a year or two I decided I'd have to find the answer on my own.

I began rummaging through the drawers and cabinets in

our home, and soon I found photos of my father and mother and eventually I found an old bank statement that had his name on it. Armed with that information, I decided that I would try to find out where he lived. It occurred to me that he might no longer be alive, but my mother's fierce reaction whenever I asked about him led me to believe that he was. There's a limit to how angry you can be with a dead person, and my mother had surpassed that limit.

Somehow, I learned that he lived in a certain city, and I got ahold of his phone number. I dialed the number but hung up as soon as someone answered.

Typically foolish fifteen-year-old that I was, I didn't stop at one attempt. Later, I learned that I called and hung up no less than fifty times.

How did I know?

My mother burst into my room, furious like never before. "Do you want to get us in trouble? Why did you call your father?"

"How do you know I called him?"

"How do I know? Because you got me in trouble! He thinks it was me who's been harassing him. He doesn't believe that it was you who called! Don't you understand that your father is not the right person to start up with?"

I began to cry bitterly. "How do you know? I didn't even know if he was still alive. You didn't tell me where he lives or if he has other children. I'm not afraid to start up with him. He's my father and I intend to ask him why he left me."

"Don't you dare!" my mother shouted.

"Why? Do I have to be afraid to start up with you, too?"

She slapped me, which she'd never done before. "Don't you talk like that to your mother, do you hear? You don't know anything. When you get older, you'll understand."

She left me alone with my thoughts.

The next day, I approached her and said quietly, "Ima, I apologize for my outburst yesterday, but I'm begging you: please tell me about my father. If you don't tell me about him, I'm afraid I won't be able to hold back from taking a trip to his house, knocking at his door and asking him why he left me, his daughter. I'm not afraid to get into any more trouble with him than I already am."

Ima thought about what I said and then said resignedly, "Okay, I'll tell you, but don't blame me later."

She carefully broke the news to me that my father was not an ordinary person. Floundering for words, she said, "He... doesn't obey the law. The police would love to get their hands on him. He does things you're not allowed to do, and many people are afraid of him."

"Are you saying he's a criminal?" I asked.

"Uh, yes," she replied.

"Is he... a thief?" I asked.

"Yes... no... not only... He's a lot more than a thief; he's a ringleader of a large network of criminals. It's really a shame you're asking so many questions; there's no reason you need to know this."

"How come he isn't in jail?" I asked.

My mother smiled sadly. "When you grow up, you'll understand that it's the small fry who sits in jail. The leaders live in regular houses and quietly issue orders. They don't even have to use words. There's no law against winking or gesturing, after all. That's why these people are never caught. The police have to content themselves with locking up their foot soldiers, but everyone knows who's behind it all."

Seeking Atonement

It wasn't easy for me to hear this. My mother had been correct to try and hide the information from me. A very difficult period followed as I struggled to reconcile myself with the fact that my father was a serious criminal who had cut off all contact with me and my mother.

◆ ◆ ◆

Over the next few years, I heard my father's name on a few occasions as people discussed the news. We had only *chareidi* newspapers at home, which never report the names of criminals, but his name was sufficiently well-known that even members of our community were familiar with it. Every time I heard someone discussing him and the crimes he'd committed, I'd shrink into myself for fear I'd be recognized as his daughter.

Baruch Hashem, that never happened.

I asked my mother at what point she had decided to leave him, and to my surprise, she said she hadn't: *he* had left *her* when she began showing an interest in being observant. He had never remarried.

I asked her why she hadn't left him when she'd learned of his illegal activities, and she explained that she had been brought up to believe that divorce is not an option. If you are fortunate to have a kind and righteous husband, you rejoice, and if you have an evil one, it's your job to help him mend his ways. True to her upbringing, she had tried her best to influence him to mend his ways, until he decided he'd had enough of her foolishness and decided to banish her to a life of poverty and need, refusing to support her or hear about his only daughter.

My mother told me that this was actually the kindest thing he'd done in his life, because by leaving her, he'd enabled me to grow up far from the type of people with whom he kept company.

"You were raised and educated in purity," she said, "and I'm glad you had no contact with him, not even once-a-month visits. Any type of a connection with him would not have done you any good," she said.

When I turned eighteen, I understood that I really had a problem. One after another friends began to celebrate their engagements, and I realized that my prospects for a decent match were bleak. My mother could barely afford our day-to-day expenses; how would she marry me off? We were poor; we had no family; and it was best not to speak of my *yichus*. I was in despair.

One day, he called my mother.

Just like that, with no advance warning. It was evening when the phone rang. My mother answered it and I saw her grow pale.

I heard her say, "Why would you want that?" then, "Okay," and then, "How did that happen?" She finished with the words, "Okay, but I'll come myself in the meantime."

She hung up the phone and began to cry bitterly.

"What's the matter?" I asked. "Who was that?"

"Your father."

"What did he want?"

"To marry me again."

"What?!"

"He wants to remarry me," she repeated.

"And what did you say?"

"I agreed."

"Tell me, Ima, are you…"

Seeking Atonement

"You won't change my mind. I was his wife and I shall remain his wife."

"After all he did to you?"

"After all he did to me."

I had never been so angry at my mother as I was then. "Where's your self-respect?" I thundered. "Someone throws you out, takes no interest in you for years on end, doesn't give you a cent in support. Then he snaps his fingers, and you go running?"

"Yes, I know, it seems crazy, but that's what I'm going to do."

"What made him suddenly think of you?"

"He told me that he's dying," she said, as if it were the most natural thing in the world.

"Is he sick?"

"It sounds like he's very, very sick. He wants to marry me before he dies."

"Why?"

"I don't know. I'll go see him tomorrow and he'll tell me."

"I'm going with you," I said.

"No, you're not," she said, ending the conversation.

She went the following day and returned with the strangest explanation I'd ever heard.

Apparently, the man (I find it hard to call him my father) had just a few weeks left to live, and with death staring him in the face, he began to fear Divine retribution. He knew that a person's sins are erased on his wedding day, so he thought it only natural to ask the wife he'd abandoned so many years ago to marry him again. This way, he could perform the mitzvah of remarrying the woman one has divorced and arrive in *Shamayim* "clean."

"And you agreed?" I asked in disbelief.

"Of course," she replied.

"You know he's not marrying you because he suddenly realized that he really always respected you or anything. He's just worried for his own fate."

"I know that well. But in any case, after his death, I'll be a widow rather than a divorcée, and that suits me better."

At least this made some sense.

A few days later, my mother remarried my father in the presence of ten people. They were married by the *rav* of the area where my father lived.

My mother had asked me if I wanted to be present, but I preferred not to. I didn't make that decision spontaneously; I really thought about it a lot before reaching the conclusion that it would be best that way. I had managed fine without my father until that point, and I didn't think I stood to gain by getting to know him.

My mother remained with him in his house to nurse him through his final illness. Apparently, he had spoken the truth about his illness, for he survived only a few weeks longer. Then he fell into a coma and died.

My mother sat *shivah*. I received a *heter* from a *rav* not to, as a result of my mother's explanation that spending time with my father's family could cause irreversible damage to my *neshamah*.

How right she was! On the one occasion that I went to console my mother, I was alarmed by the type of people I met. They were completely alien to my world; tough and frightening, though they treated me with respect bordering on reverence. I had the feeling they were regarding me as heir to the king of crime. A flood of people came to the house to console the mourners, each dropping off an envelope filled

Seeking Atonement

with cash. Apparently, this was a custom they had picked up from the Italian mafia.

I fled from there as quickly as possible. It was a place I wanted nothing to do with.

My mother completed *shivah* and returned home.

On that same day, she told me that we were moving.

This is where the third part of my life began.

Although I had been furious with my mother for acting like a dishrag, she had in fact displayed great courage. Thinking of my future, she'd informed her ex-husband that his "atonement" would cost him all the child support payments he'd never made on my behalf. She'd also told him that he'd have to pay for an apartment so that I could marry a *ben Torah* "who might be able to achieve atonement for your sins with his prayers."

He hadn't attempted to argue. He issued an order to the right person and a large sum of money was immediately deposited in my mother's bank account. Only then had she agreed to marry him.

Apparently, thoughts of repentance had stricken him at death's door. He acknowledged the fact that his life had been the epitome of evil and then he did his best to correct whatever he could. My mother spoke with him about me and her description apparently caused him to truly regret his having cut me out of his life. She told me that he spent the next few days crying tears of regret for what he had done. He asked her to pass on his request for forgiveness for having abandoned me, but she told him what she had once told me: that the greatest *chesed* he'd ever done for me was to allow me to be raised and educated in the *chareidi* world with no connection to him or his world. Although my mother was very respectful to him, she was direct, honest and fearless.

And now I've reached the final part of my story.

My father kept his word and left us a large inheritance so that we could live a good life and lack nothing. My mother had no problem accepting the money: she said he had been obligated to support us all the years we hadn't heard from him, and now he had simply repaid his debt in one lump sum. Say what you will about my mother, she has an a very original outlook on life.

I received a good *shidduch*, which unfortunately says something rather uncomplimentary about our community: As long as you have money, finding a *shidduch* is not a problem, no matter the circumstances. You might prefer to delete this line, but you can't erase the truth it contains. (Apparently, I inherited my mother's penchant for speaking her mind.)

I got a great husband from a wonderful family. Over the years, we had children who attended the finest schools, and I recently married off my daughter to a *ben Torah*. I try to use the money from the man who twice married my mother (notice the lengths to which I go to avoid calling him my father) only for good causes such as *chinuch* and securing our children's future.

My mother is already elderly, but still very sharp. She's had a hard life, but she says the compensation she received — me — was worth everything. And truly, at least the second half of her life has been filled with *nachas* and joy.

A Letter to Daddy and Mommy

Two sisters contend with a difficult dilemma.

Their parents bicker inappropriately. They cannot bring themselves to speak with their parents about how this is affecting them, so they decide to write them a letter and send it in the mail.

Now that they are themselves mothers, one of them decided to send this letter to every parent in Klal Yisrael.

On one of your radio programs, Rabbi Walder, I heard a twenty-year-old young man relate that his parents argue excessively in front of their children. You suggested that he and his married sister write their parents a letter telling them how their quarrels affected them as children and asking them with all due respect to stop their behavior for the benefit of the other children.

My husband heard this and told me that in his opinion, your advice was inappropriate, because children should never, ever criticize their parents, under any circumstances.

I regarded him in silence for a moment, and then suddenly,

I burst into tears. My husband was alarmed. He couldn't understand what had elicited such a strong reaction in me.

He tried to encourage me to share with him what it was that had affected me so, but I told him I needed to calm down first. He was very concerned.

Then my sister called. "Did you hear?" she asked.

"Yes," I replied.

"And what did it remind you of?"

"The same thing it reminded you of," I replied.

"You sound sad," she said. "I was actually very pleased."

We had always been different, my sister and I.

After I calmed down, I told my husband the story. With his encouragement, I decided to write to you about the memories that surfaced in my mind as a result of your advice.

🎬 🎬 🎬

We grew up in a wonderful home, me and my five siblings. Our parents were good to us: warm, loving and attentive.

They loved us dearly, but they bickered terribly between them. Most of the time, they were like any other couple, but when they quarreled — it was disastrous.

They would hurl a stream of angry, hurtful words at one another, spewing insults and threats that made us cringe in fear.

This would be followed by two or three days of thunderous silence accompanied by glares that were no less frightening than words. Then it was over and they would be back to normal.

The situation was terribly confusing to us.

My sister and I were then nine and ten years old, and I remember nearly every outburst. They occurred about once or twice a month, and to our young eyes, they were the same

A Letter to Daddy and Mommy

every time: the parents that we loved, admired and trusted, suddenly began behaving like... well, it was hard to say like what, because in our wonderful, insular neighborhood, no one we knew behaved like that. Maybe like a drunkard on Purim or a driver with road rage.

In our own home we witnessed verbal abuse that frightened us terribly and ate away our respect for them.

We were terrified that our parents would divorce and then we'd be forced to choose between them. We loved them both equally and could not bear to think of such a situation.

One day, after a stormy argument that caused us to run to our room, hide under our desk and embrace one another, my sister said, "Do you know that in the Holocaust, this is how the Jews sat in bunkers, hiding from the Nazis?"

"You shouldn't talk like that!" I exclaimed.

My sister began to cry, and I hugged her even more tightly. "We've got to put a stop to this," I told her.

"How?" she asked.

"I'm going to write them a letter," I declared.

When the argument was over, we emerged from under the desk. I took out a sheet of paper, and began to write.

Dear Daddy and Mommy, I wrote.

We, (here I write my name and my sister's), are writing to ask you to stop fighting and hating each other, because it scares us to see you this way. We're afraid you're going to divorce and leave us alone. We're embarrassed and sad that you fight so much. Can't you get along?

Please, Daddy and Mommy, do us a favor and stop fighting. Maybe you should go to Savta and ask her to decide which of you is right.

We decorated the letter and envelope, walked to the local post office to purchase a stamp, and placed the letter in the mailbox.

Don't ask me why we didn't simply place the letter in our home mailbox. I have no idea. Maybe I thought it was the law, or maybe I thought that only this way could I be sure that the letter would actually arrive.

Two days later, the letter arrived. I saw my father come in with the open envelope in his hands. I pretended not to have noticed a thing. My mother wanted to serve him dinner, but he said, "I have to discuss something with you." And they went into the bedroom.

My sister and I looked at each other but didn't dare say a word. We knew they were talking about the letter, and we hoped for the best.

They came out of their bedroom and called us to the dinner table as if nothing had happened.

From that point on, our lives changed. My parents never fought again, at least not in front of us. Since that day, I never heard another shout or insult from either of them. Once, half a year after the letter, my mother began to say something, but my father said, "Let's put this discussion off for later."

And then he added: "I don't want to receive any more letters…"

And he winked at us.

That's my story, and after I told it to my husband, he no longer thought your advice was inappropriate. At first, I thought you would want to print this story in *Kidspeak*, but

A Letter to Daddy and Mommy

perhaps you would be doing the public more of a service by printing it in *People Speak*, so that parents would realize how detrimental parental fights can be to their children.

I'm not an esteemed *chinuch* personage and I can't say whether or not it is permissible to tell children such a story. I remember that you asked the caller how old he was, and only when you heard that he was over the age of eighteen did you suggest that he speak with his parents or write them a letter.

Perhaps it is wrong to encourage children to criticize their parents. I know one thing: the respectful and loving letter I wrote to my parents changed the lives of every single one of us in our home.

Publicizing this story might help all those children who see their parents fighting and can't come up with a way to stop it. If you are such a parent, read the letter my sister and I wrote and pretend your children wrote it to you... because that's exactly how they feel.

A Stab to the Heart

A teenage girl is abandoned suddenly by her good friend at the behest of her friend's family.
This is a heart-wrenching story of friendship and separation, and the delicate dilemma of which is more harmful.

My story begins more than thirty years ago, but it's relevant today as well.

My parents were very refined people. My father was a typically aloof *Yekke* while my mother was a typically proud Polish woman. They were very cultured. There was never any screaming or arguing in our house, which was always neat as a pin. Classical music played in the background and we had a library full of thick, boring books.

Of course, I studied piano at a conservatory, not because I loved music but because that was the accepted thing to do. I was very polite and I knew just what to say at which occasion (and when not to speak at all).

We lived in a respectable neighborhood in Jerusalem that

originally had a secular majority but slowly began filling with *chareidi* families like our own. Well, not *exactly* like our own, because although we both observed Torah and mitzvos, our culture included piano, literature and classical music, while theirs most decidedly did not.

At first, my parents were very tolerant of our new neighbors. I never heard them utter a word against them, even though they were Yerushalmis who wore different hats and long suits and had customs somewhat different from ours.

The music played in their homes was not classical at all, and although my parents never told us what they thought of that music, their facial expressions made it abundantly clear.

With each passing year, I saw their tolerance toward the new population filling the neighborhood diminish. They had plenty of criticism: the new neighbors didn't watch their children carefully enough, nor did they provide them with a well-rounded education. It was a fact that not a single one of them played the piano. True, there were some neighbors who played the drums or the clarinet, but it was pointless to even mention that to my parents. Drums? The clarinet? Maybe in Africa that was something to be proud of. Not in their cultured world.

As a child, I was drawn to our Yerushalmi neighbors. The very same characteristics that were the subject of my parents' disapproval — entranced me. I had only two sisters, whereas Rivky and Freidy and Surele, all of whom lived in our building, had eight or nine siblings each. At the tender age of eight, I longed to be able to push a baby carriage with a sibling inside, just like my newfound friends.

I spent a lot of time in the neighbors' homes. Although my parents explained the reason for their disapproval in a few short sentences, they did not forbid me to go. After all, no one ever displayed anger or raised his voice in our home.

I was simply attracted by the other culture I saw. I was drawn to families who laughed and sang and danced together, and whose members sometimes shouted in annoyance. One day, I told my mother that our house was like a graveyard in the middle of a playground. She didn't speak to me for a week after that comment.

❦ ❦ ❦

While we're on the topic of silence, I'd like to make a comment. Many parenting experts and child psychologists talk about how important it is to refrain from shouting at a child. I want them and everyone else to know that silence can be ten times worse. There were times when I longed for my father or mother to shout at me or show some sign of annoyance; anything would have been better than their habit of simply ignoring me. *That* was suffering. I don't blame my parents; their culture was one of restraint. Restraint is a good thing because it holds a person's temper in check, but it must be taken into account that it holds a parent's natural feelings of love and compassion in check, too.

Upon completing elementary school, I attended a different high school from the one my neighbors attended (a Yiddish-language school). This situation resulted in a very painful separation from my friends; in fact, I would say that the pain of this separation was the worst pain I have endured in my life. My friends were my entire world — especially Rivky.

Rivky was my very best friend. I used to sit and talk to her for hours, and we became very close. Although I came from a completely different type of home, her parents allowed me to befriend their daughter after they got to know me and were satisfied that my parents had educated me properly.

A Stab to the Heart

Interestingly, I was the one who *davened* more fervently and was more careful with my performance of mitzvos, while Rivky tended to be somewhat lax. Her parents saw that I had a good influence on her and approved of our friendship.

Thanks to Rivky, I was able to push a baby carriage at the age of eight. It wasn't my brother inside, but I was able to pretend… More sisters and brothers were born in quick succession and Rivky and I liked nothing better than feeding them and caring for them like little mommies.

Rivky's father was a happy, friendly person who showered his family with warmth and love. Her mother was by nature more reserved, but in her own quiet way, she spread warmth and demonstrated proper values.

Rivky's family was far from wealthy, but their home was filled with joy. Their home was completely closed to foreign influences, yet I never felt that they were any less intelligent than my family.

A few days after I was accepted to a more open high school, I shared the news with Rivky. She asked me whether my decision to attend that school was final. "Of course," I replied. "I tried very hard to get into this high school." For the next few weeks, she avoided me, but in my naiveté, I didn't realize anything was amiss.

The day before high school began, a letter was delivered to my home. I opened it and immediately recognized Rivky's handwriting.

My parents forbid me to be your friend, I read. *I have no choice but to ask you not to try and contact me. It could cause a lot of trouble. Your friendship has meant a lot to me. Rivka.*

To this day, I can't understand how I survived that moment. I was in total shock. It was like a huge calamity had befallen me.

With the innocence of a young girl, I ran quickly to Rivky's house to speak with her. Her older sister opened the door and asked me, as if I was a stranger: "Yes?"

"I need to speak with Rivky," I said.

"Weren't you told that you should no longer speak with her?"

"I was, but..."

"No buts. You're not friends anymore. You'd better get used to that," she said, closing the door in my face.

Rivky's sister had always been jealous of our friendship.

I was shell-shocked. I sat there on the steps, crying, until my sister happened to pass by and took me home.

For the next few days I hardly ate, spoke or slept. I spent all day long looking out the window, waiting to see Rivky. When I didn't see her, I began haunting the area near her house.

Finally, one day I met her and looked her in the eye. She seemed very sad. She flashed her acknowledgment with her eyes but was afraid to talk. A moment later, she was gone.

I went through an unbearably difficult time. I felt I would be better off dead. I went to school but barely ate. My parents, at their wits' end, had no idea what to say to me. I wanted them to force me to eat, to soothe me, console me, or at least rail against Rivky and her family. But they couldn't understand why I was behaving like this because of a friend they had never liked. Their ordered world did not include deep, emotional bonds, and by extension, not the pain of separation either. They couldn't understand that I was different from them, that I had given my heart and soul to my friend and was unable to cope with the sudden severance of a deep emotional connection. They could not fathom the cause for my depression.

The next emotion I felt was hatred. I hated Rivky by day and I hated her at night. I hated thinking about her and I hated missing her. I hated the gifts she had bought me and the pictures we'd taken together.

Then I hated myself for having given my heart and soul to someone who had abandoned me so cruelly and cared not a whit for my feelings.

My parents sent me to a psychologist, and with her help, I was able to begin functioning normally again, but I was lonely and hurt. I still spent a large portion of my day dreaming about the girl who used to be my best friend.

Almost a full year passed this way. It was a year that left my soul badly scarred.

Toward the end of the year, I suffered a terrible blow.

My father suffered a severe heart attack and had to be hospitalized. My mother was forced to stay in the hospital while my sisters and I stayed home alone. We were completely unprepared for a situation like this.

The neighbors immediately came to our aid. They sent food and inquired how we were faring and how our father was feeling. After a while, the doctors told my parents that his condition necessitated surgery abroad.

This was a serious complication. We had no extended family. Our neighbors discussed the situation and decided that each of us children would be taken in by a different family until my parents returned.

Since no one knew what had transpired between me and

Rivky's family, no one objected when I was placed with her family.

I knew nothing of these plans.

We accompanied our parents to the airport. I said goodbye with tears in my eyes, knowing there was a chance I'd never see my father again.

My father was teary-eyed and choked up with emotion, a situation to which I was completely unaccustomed. The strangeness of it all only exacerbated my own emotional upheaval and fear.

They left and we returned home.

When we returned, a neighbor was waiting for us. He told us that each of us would be staying with a different family and then simply led us each to the home of the family where we would stay.

He brought me to… Rivky's house.

Before I could say, "I can't stay here," he led me inside and shut the door.

Rivky's mother smiled and spoke to me as if it were the most natural thing in the world for me to be there. "You'll sleep in Rivky's room," she said, leading me to a room that was overwhelmingly saturated with memories.

I felt trapped. Rivky's room was both the most beloved and most hated place in the world; I had enjoyed many a wonderful time there, but the memory of those times had caused me endless angst. Coming on top of the difficulty of my parents' trip abroad, the emotional overload was too much to bear.

Rivky breezed into the room and said brightly, "Hi, how are you?"

A Stab to the Heart

I opened my mouth but no sound came out. Instead, I burst into tears and was overcome by heartrending sobs.

Rivky stared at me, terribly uncomfortable, and tried to speak. "I'm not to blame for what happened. Nor is it my parents' fault. My school didn't want to accept me because they'd heard I was friendly with a girl from a family that didn't belong to our community. *Shidduchim* for our entire family were being endangered. I had no choice but to obey my parents in order to protect my family."

I did not respond. There was no point. There were no words to express my pain, so I simply continued crying.

A long time passed. I wept until nighttime and continued sobbing even after I was in bed.

I heard her calling my name in the darkness.

I cried on.

She called my name again.

When I didn't respond, she said, "I must explain to you what I went through. I was shattered to pieces, too, but I had no choice. Please understand."

I didn't understand. To my mind, nothing could justify such behavior. How could anyone ignore another human being's feelings like that?

※ ※ ※

For a few days, we slept in the same room. Rivky kept trying to appease me but I maintained a stony silence, unable to cope with the terrible thing that had been done to me.

On the fifth night, when she spoke to me and explained to me for the umpteenth time what had pushed her parents to this decision, I burst out, "And what about me? Wasn't I a factor here? Didn't I deserve to be presented with the facts, consulted about how to deal with the situation? Couldn't you at least have explained the situation so that I didn't feel like you were chucking me aside because I was a vile and terrible creature? Did you think of me as an inanimate object, a chair or a rug to be used and then tossed out with the trash?"

For the first time, she was silent. She didn't know what to say. I told her how terribly I had suffered, how my trust in people had been completely shattered, about the terrible thoughts that had tormented me. Finally, she began to understand what I had gone through.

"You were the only person I ever really opened up to," I wept. "How could you have done that to me?"

She had no answer for me. She apologized for the way our friendship had ended, without any explanation or preparation on her part. "Please understand," she said to me. "The school you go to is *treif* by our standards. My father's a good person, but when it comes to our principles, he's completely uncompromising."

That I could understand. I had always respected the way they were steadfast in their adherence to their principles. In hindsight, I realized that it was the fact that they had allowed their daughter to befriend me in the first place that was unusual (even though I attended one of the most distinguished schools in Yerushalayim), rather than their decision to force her to cut off all contact with me. Still, I bore a grudge in my heart for the manner in which it had been done.

And then I remembered something that had been niggling at me. "Tell me, how is it that your parents agreed to have me stay at your house?"

She thought for a moment and said, "In a situation like this, you don't make calculations."

I knew her well enough to know that while this was the truth, it wasn't the whole truth. "I could easily have stayed with a different family," I pointed out. "Or I could have been placed in a different room, not with you."

She was silent for a long moment and then she said, "I was expelled from my school."

She related that there had been a period during which she'd veered off the proper *derech*. After that, there was no going back to her old school — not that she had any interest in doing so.

Many people, *rabbanim* and *chinuch* personalities, tried to speak with her, but she was very stubborn. She crossed many boundaries and fell very far.

One day, her father came to her room and began to cry. He said not a word; he neither rebuked her nor showed any anger. He just wept and wept, and after a long silence, explained to her how badly he longed to have her maintain a connection with them and not go off the *derech*.

That talk affected her very deeply, and she promised to do everything in her power not to get swept even further away.

Thereafter, they had many such talks, and one day, she told him: "Do you know what sustains me? Aside from the *chinuch* you gave me and the things I learned in school, my friend — the one you made me cut off all contact with, because she wasn't 'religious enough' — she infused me with real *yiras Shamayim*. She had a very strong positive influence on me, and she still does. And you took her from me."

Her father sighed and said, "Perhaps we made a mistake. Hashem knows that our intentions were pure. We acted according to the principles of *chinuch* transmitted from generation to generation in our community. Maybe it was He Who sent her to you, but we failed to see that. I see now that your friendship was stronger than our decision to separate you."

"A few days after that conversation," Rivky told me, "one

of the neighbors came and told us about your father's illness and your parents' upcoming trip. My father had no doubts. He asked that you be placed with us."

❧   ❧   ❧

That's the story, and it's not over yet.

Our friendship has grown and blossomed and continues to this day.

My father regained his strength and enjoyed a number of years of good health thereafter.

We are both happily married. My husband learns in *kollel*. Her husband works, but he sets aside time for Torah study. I think our story testifies to the marvelous way in which Hashem runs the world. He orchestrates events in order to help us with our children's *chinuch* and other affairs, as well.

Today, I can analyze this story from a mature vantage point. I don't judge Rivky's parents as harshly as before; I can appreciate the way they perceived the situation at the time.

In their place, would I do the same? I might try to prevent a friendship I perceived as inappropriate from developing in the first place. I certainly would not cut off a friendship in such a cruel and hurtful manner. True, I have the benefit of hindsight; I know firsthand how much damage their decision caused both me and their daughter. Had they known, they certainly would not have behaved the way they did.

Still, there's a lesson here that I feel is of utmost importance. Separating two *neshamos* from one another is like cutting flesh. If ever you feel your daughter's friendship with someone else must be stopped, be aware that the surgery must be done with utmost skill. Realize that both girls could be deeply scarred if the situation is not handled properly.

14

Covered for Life

A secular Israeli family moves to New York and forms a connection with the chareidi community there.

Slowly, the family embraces Yiddishkeit, but there's one thing that presents a true obstacle for the woman. She just can't bring herself to cover her hair.

When she finally takes the plunge, with great difficulty, something happens that turns into one of the most talked about stories in New York.

I live in New York and I've read all your books, including the one I liked best, *Behind the Mask*.

Chances are you've already heard the story I'm about to write, as it's very well-known in the Jewish community here in New York, but I heard a few women saying that this story ought to be written up in *People Speak*, so I decided to hurry up and write it in the hope that I'd be the first. Also, I am familiar with the story firsthand.

A few years ago, a family from Israel moved to New York. We didn't really know them at first, because Israeli families don't usually integrate that well into the community — or rather, the community is not overly welcoming to Israelis. This is not because we look askance at leaving Eretz Yisrael, but rather because we look askance at the Israeli personality. I hope you won't be insulted by the fact that many Americans feel this way about Israelis, just as I don't feel hurt by the fact that Israelis don't have the greatest affinity for Americans. I'd say we're "even-Steven" in that respect.

In any case, this particular family got stuck in the middle. I'm not sure why, but they didn't integrate with the community of ex-Israelis, nor did they join the regular community.

The truth is that many Israelis attempt, at first, to snub their fellow expatriates and fit in with the regular community. Most of the time, such attempts fail dismally. Even if everyone is polite and friendly, no one invites the ex-Israelis to weddings or other occasions. Before long, new immigrants realize that it just won't work.

In the end, they find their place, though. Believe me, there are so many former Israelis here that they have plenty of room to fit in.

But the family I'm talking about simply did not integrate with the expatriate community, nor were they daunted by the fact that they weren't invited to the regular community's affairs.

At the time I got to know them, they were not religious, but they weren't completely secular, either. Like many ex-Israelis, they drew a little bit closer to Judaism after arriving in America. I know it sounds strange, but many secular Israelis feel very Jewish in Israel because they are surrounded by Jews wherever they go. In America, however, they suddenly feel the need to prove their Jewishness to themselves, and they do this by showing up for *tefillos* and sending their children to Sunday school (those that don't attend Jewish schools). Seeing their non-Jewish neighbors, who look completely secular, proudly attend church gives them a jolt, and they feel the need to attend services at a synagogue in order to establish their own identity. It's sad, but it's a part of *galus* that Jews have to learn from the non-Jews.

Since this family lived quite close to our neighborhood, they began frequenting our shul, and that's how we met.

The first time I met Sivan, she had arrived at the synagogue dressed immodestly and someone had said something to her about it. She responded by bursting into tears, and I and another few women soothed her but explained that there was a certain dress code for attending services in an Orthodox synagogue. She had never heard of the word "Orthodox" before, which isn't surprising, really, considering that the Reform and Conservative movements do not have a large following in Israel, whereas in America, hundreds of thousands of Jews are affiliated with these movements.

It was only after we explained to her the existential difference between Reform Jews and Orthodox ones that she recalled having visited a Reform synagogue. She hadn't liked it there, though; it had reminded her of a church. "If I wanted to pray in a church," she said, "I'd join my neighbors. But I'm Jewish." And she made up her mind to attend the following week dressed modestly and wearing a headscarf.

Although her "modest" clothing was still not up to our standards, and her headscarf left more revealed than was proper, we decided to draw her closer in a kind and pleasant way.

Seeing her sincerity, we began to invite her to our homes. Slowly but surely, she and her husband strengthened their commitment to Torah observance, and soon they switched their children to Jewish schools.

Sivan took the lead in all matters Jewish, while her husband, like so many others, at first went along with her just to keep her happy and off his back. At some point, however — I think it was when he began studying *Gemara* — he suddenly picked up the pace and before we knew it, he was growing a beard and wearing a suit and hat.

Sivan, too, made radical changes to her wardrobe, but there was one thing she just could not bring herself to do: cover her hair.

"I just feel so weird," she said. "I can't do it. I mean, I can put on a scarf for services, but in the street? I just can't."

We didn't push her, but she knew it was entirely inappropriate for a woman whose children were attending *chareidi* schools not to cover her hair.

When we mentioned the possibility of covering her hair with a wig, she told us an amusing story about the first time she had even heard that *chareidi* women wear wigs.

She told us that at her former workplace in Israel, she had know a *chareidi* woman, who had, at some point, said about another colleague, "She isn't *chareidi*. She doesn't cover her hair."

"Why do you say that?" Sivan had asked her. "You don't cover your hair, either."

The *chareidi* colleague had looked hurt. "Of course I do," she'd protested.

"Is this some kind of a joke?" Sivan had asked. "Look at yourself in a mirror. Maybe you forgot your hat at home and didn't notice?"

Covered for Life

The *chareidi* woman suddenly realized that Sivan was truly clueless. "Haven't you ever heard of a wig?" she'd asked.

No, she hadn't.

Her friend had then explained to her the principle behind covering one's hair. "All *chareidi* women cover their hair," she'd explained. "Some wear headscarves while others wear wigs. In both cases, their own hair is hidden."

Sivan had asked many questions, eventually leading up to: What's the difference between a woman's own hair and that of a non-Jewish woman from India?

Her friend had replied that *halachah* mandates that a married woman cover her hair. "Some *rabbanim* do indeed forbid the wearing of wigs for the reason you pointed out, but most, especially the Ashkenazi ones, permit it."

Sivan refused to consider wearing a headscarf, and I didn't blame her, because in the area where she lived no one else did. But a wig didn't seem like an acceptable alternative to her, either.

A few months passed. One day, she called and told me she was prepared to go to a wig stylist. "I've got to try," she told me.

I was very excited. I immediately set up an appointment with a well-known wig stylist and explw`ained the situation. The wig stylist had a full appointment schedule, but under the circumstances, she agreed to squeeze her in. I accompanied her there and we chose a wig.

The following Shabbos, she came to shul with her wig and received tremendous praise from all the ladies in the women's section. The elderly woman, who had reprimanded her the first time she'd come, embraced her warmly. It was a very special and moving scene.

A week later, Sivan went to the bank to deposit her monthly salary, which she had received in cash.

She was standing in line when a huge man in a ski mask burst inside, fired a shot at the ceiling and shouted, "This is a stick up! Hands in the air!"

He instructed the lone teller to empty her cash box. In the meantime, he began collecting the wallets of everyone in line. Sivan was terribly frightened, but of course she didn't dream of objecting. Having no choice, she handed over her wallet containing the few thousand dollars she'd been planning to deposit. Aside from her distress over the loss of her money, she was quaking with fear that the robber might fire another shot.

The robber collected the money from the teller and was about to leave. Sivan began breathing a bit easier, but just then, the wail of a siren sounded from outside. Someone had alerted the police, and whereas previously it had seemed there was a chance the robbery would be completed without bloodshed, now everyone in the bank was in mortal danger.

The police surrounded the building. The robber's eyes darted back and forth like those of a wounded, trapped animal. Suddenly, his gaze rested on Sivan. He approached her, held his gun to her temple, and began dragging her toward the exit. She was to be his human shield.

He left the bank, shouting, "If anyone tries to stop me, I'll pull the trigger!"

The policemen stood there, unable to do a thing. The robber dragged Sivan to an old car parked on the opposite side of the street and ordered her to open the door.

"But you're holding my hands," Sivan pointed out.

The robber hesitated for a moment and then, with one hand still holding the gun tightly to her temple, switched his

Covered for Life

other hand from Sivan's hands to her head. Clutching a handful of hair, he said, "Now open the door."

Sivan reached up, loosened the clips on her wig, bent down, and fled, covering her hair with the scarf she had been wearing around her neck as she ran.

The robber stared in shock at what seemed to be Sivan's hair in his hand. He couldn't understand where the rest of her had disappeared to.

He left this world still in a state of utter confusion as bullets riddled his body. The moment the officer in charge saw Sivan fleeing, he gave the order to open fire on the armed assailant before he would have a chance to injure innocent citizens.

The robber fell to the ground, his gun clattering to the floor. Only Sivan's wig remained clutched in his hand.

Sivan arrived at my house with her head wrapped in her woolen scarf, quaking with fear and excitement.

The following Shabbos, a *seudas hoda'ah* was held to thank Hashem for the miracle He had performed. Sivan recited *birkas hagomel* from the women's section and the entire congregation answered *Amen*.

If Sivan still had any lingering doubts about whether she had done the right thing in covering her hair despite all her reservations, this episode removed them all!

The Reward for Humiliation

Humiliation is one of the hardest things for a person to contend with.

Public humiliation is an exceptionally difficult form of torture, but it can be harnessed into a positive experience that can bring incredible benefits in its wake.

Hard to believe? Consider the following story...

I would like to tell you a terrible, shocking story to which I was witness from beginning to end.

It began at an evening for women, to benefit a particular organization. Hundreds of women were in attendance and matters were proceeding as they always did at such events, with speeches, booths and a Chinese auction.

At some point, the name of a certain speaker was announced. Her name was not that well-known, but the topic she was to address sounded interesting; so slowly but steadily, women began streaming into the auditorium to find seats.

The speaker made her way to the podium.

The Reward for Humiliation

She stood there waiting for the audience to quiet down. Anyone who has ever been at a women's event knows this can take awhile...

Suddenly, a tall woman approached her and began shouting, "I recognize you! A few years ago, you insulted me in public and ruined my life! You humiliated me in public!"

All this took place in front of hundreds of women.

The speaker blanched. "B-b-but I don't know you," she stammered.

"Well, it happened many years ago, but I haven't forgotten," the woman thundered. She grabbed the microphone and announced, "It's forbidden to listen to this woman! Many years ago, she ruined my life by humiliating me in public! She deserves to be publicly condemned!"

One of the organizers of the event stepped forward and asked the woman to stop, but she paid her no attention. Another two women tried to wrest the microphone from her hand, but she was stronger than them. She pushed them away and continued shouting insults against the speaker into the microphone.

Although the audience was shocked by the woman's behavior, it must be noted that she seemed very sincere. It appeared that she had, indeed, once been terribly hurt by the speaker.

Everyone felt awful for the speaker, who looked as though she had been flogged and dragged through the mud. How can a person bear such humiliation, especially as she had just been about to address a large crowd?

Members of the audience began shouting at the tall woman to keep quiet. Suddenly, the speaker fled the room, crying bitterly.

A number of women, myself among them, tried to comfort the speaker even as her attacker continued besmirching her. I offered her a cup of water. Suddenly, through her tears, the speaker said, "Do me a favor, please. Can you call Rochel X?"

"Rochel X? W-w-why?" We didn't understand what she had to do with anything.

"It's a matter of *pikuach nefesh*," the speaker insisted. "Announce on the microphone that Rochel X should please come here."

We stared at one another, afraid the traumatic experience had muddled her, but she repeated her request, more insistently this time. "Call her and then you'll understand why."

I went to a different microphone and announced, "Rochel X, please make you way to the entrance of the hall immediately."

I returned to the speaker, who was still weeping bitterly, and together we waited for Rochel X, who indeed came hurrying over a moment later. "Is someone looking for me?" she asked.

"Yes, I am," replied the speaker. "I'm your mother's friend." Suddenly, she placed her hands on Rochel's head and said, "At this time of great humiliation for me, as my distress reaches all the way to the Heavenly Throne, I request, no plead, that you be blessed with a child within the year. Please, Hashem, take all the terrible humiliation that I am suffering and convert them into merits for Rochel *bas* so-and-so."

We stared at one another in disbelief. Rochel seemed very uncomfortable and left the area. The speaker, for her part, seemed infused with newfound strength. She wiped her eyes and said, "I just want to make it clear that the woman is making a mistake. I have no idea what she's talking about."

The Reward for Humiliation

In the meantime, the tall woman was still talking. Her microphone had been shut off, but her voice was loud enough to be heard without it.

One of the organizers, a dynamic and assertive woman, approached the podium and asked her, "Tell me, do you know the name of the woman you're attacking?"

"I don't know what her name is today," the woman said, "but her maiden name was Cohen. She was our Bnos leader, and she..." and she launched into yet another recount of the humiliation she had suffered at the hands of Miss Cohen.

In the meantime, upon the request of the organizer, the speaker dug through her purse, withdrew her driver's license and handed it to the organizer.

The organizer approached the woman who had seized control of the event, took the microphone from her hand and signaled someone to switch it back on. Then she said, "Her maiden name is not Cohen; it's Stern. I think this must be a case of mistaken identity. Our speaker probably looks very much like the woman who wronged you, but it's not her."

For the first time, the woman fell silent. She grabbed the driver's license and examined it from both sides. Then she turned to the speaker and said, "So you're not Miriam Cohen (name has been changed)?"

"No, I'm not. My name was never Cohen."

"Maybe she's your sister?"

The audience laughed, and the woman realized how foolish she sounded.

"I'm sorry. I must have made a mistake," the woman said, returning to her place.

The audience now turned on her. "You should be ashamed of yourself! Ask her forgiveness! How dare you humiliate someone about to address a crowd without even making sure you had the right person?"

The woman was extremely uncomfortable now. She didn't know what to do with herself. But then we heard the speaker say, "Let's not repeat the same mistake of publicly humiliating someone, especially since the entire situation may have an unexpected benefit..."

The audience fell silent and waited for an explanation, but the speaker just began the address she had prepared. It was a wonderful speech, and after she had finished and left, the women at the event began discussing what had transpired.

Of course, the "attacker" left the hall immediately.

I made up my mind to keep tabs on the participants of the story. I wrote down the name of the speaker and that of the woman she had blessed.

I learned that Rochel X had been childless for twelve years. Just as in the most unrealistic stories, she gave birth to a healthy baby boy ten months after the speaker's blessing.

When I next had occasion to meet the speaker, I told her that I was one of the women who had heard her bless Rochel and that I saw a direct connection between her blessing and the miracle that had transpired. I asked her to explain how she had thought of Rochel at a time of such great distress.

At first, she tried to evade my question and pretend that Rochel's miracle had nothing to do with her, but I persisted. Finally, she softened and told me the following:

"It is written that when a person is suffering, his soul is more connected to the *Kisei Hakavod*. Humiliation is the worst form of suffering a human being can endure. It is with good reason that Chazal compared a person who humiliates

The Reward for Humiliation

his friend in public to a murderer. A person who is being humiliated feels as though his blood is being spilled.

"That is how I felt when the woman began attacking me in public. It was sheer torture. I tried to think how I could use the suffering I was experiencing to help someone else, and I suddenly thought of Rochel, my friend's daughter. I had seen her earlier in the evening, so I knew she was in the hall. I blessed her with all my heart, and apparently, my blessing reached all the way to the Heavenly Throne and *Hakadosh Baruch Hu* decided to honor it."

That's the story. There are two reasons I decided to write it to you.

First, I want to tell people in search of *segulos* about the awesome potential of a blessing from someone who has been humiliated, especially if he chose to remain silent in the face of the humiliation rather than return fire.

An additional lesson can be learned by those who suffer humiliation — either as a one-time experience or on an ongoing basis — as their reputation or honor is attacked. You have tremendous power to pray for and bless others. If you should find yourself in such a situation, perceive the situation in a different way: set out on a mission to help as many people as you can, for your blessings now carry more weight than those of an average person. Utilize the situation to bless your family members and anyone you know who is in need of a *yeshuah*. This will infuse you with newfound strength to deal with your own difficulties, and besides, "He who prays for his friend is answered first."

16

Peace at Home

Unfortunately, disagreements among neighbors who live in the same building are all too common.

Sometimes, however, when disagreements turn into full-fledged battles, it can destroy the lives of both families.

When two families are embroiled in an argument, they don't realize that they are actually hurting themselves.

My story begins fifteen years ago. I was twelve years old when my parents became embroiled in an argument with the neighbors who lived across the hall from us.

We lived on the top floor of the building, and as such had the option of building an addition into the roof. The neighbors decided to build into their side of the roof. All the neighbors in the building, including ourselves, had signed off on the renovation and they received the necessary building permits. However, they deviated considerably from the amount of space they had been allotted, which encroached on our side of the roof. My parents had also planned to build into the roof, and they were understandably upset about it. They took the

Peace at Home

neighbors to a *din Torah*. The neighbors refused to show up and the *beis din* served them with a *seruv* that caused them much humiliation but did not change the situation. Finally, my parents were granted permission to sue them in court.

The court obligated them to either demolish what they had built or pay us a few thousand dollars in compensation. They chose to pay, but at the time, they lacked the funds. My parents filed a petition to have liens placed on their property and their income, and soon the story became an ugly mess of legal documents flying back and forth. Many people tried to persuade my parents to back down, but they refused.

As a boy and later a teen, I took an active part in all this, arguing bitterly with the neighbors' children. Soon the entire neighborhood knew about the argument, and both the adults and the children took sides.

In the end, from a legal point of view, we won. We received every last cent of the compensation money. But woe to such a victory, as the hatred remained. From the time I was twelve years old, our family lived in a cloud of hatred that spread to the entire building and even the entire neighborhood.

This is the type of hatred that's felt in every limb of one's body, and the flames were constantly being fanned because we lived across the hall from each other. Imagine, also, the uncomfortable moments when our neighbor would leave his house just as we were stepping out of ours and we would bump into each other in the hallway. It was an unbearable situation of tension, anger and hatred.

The hatred grew even worse with time. Attempts were made to ruin my reputation in *yeshivah ketanah*, and again in *yeshivah gedolah*, and all that, we later learned, was just "target practice" for when I began *shidduchim*.

Many *shidduch* suggestions stopped cold as soon as the other party began asking information about my family and heard about the ugly fight between us and the neighbors. Some made an attempt to find out who was right and contacted our neighbors, who painted us as evil incarnate.

The most painful part was that the terrible things they said about us were, in fact, true. In other words, they basically reported that we had persecuted them mercilessly, forcing them to pay us when they could ill afford it and causing them great humiliation. It was all true, except that from our point of view, it wasn't really that cruel. After all, they were the ones who had done as they pleased without a second thought. They were the ones who had cheated us out of space that was rightfully ours, thinking they could get away with it after the walls were up. They had practically forced my parents to behave as they had. We explained all that to *shadchanim*, but they said, "You have a point, but when you saw a Jewish family suffering like that, how could you remain so hardhearted?"

We, for our part, did not remain silent. We told people how we had readily signed our consent to their construction, and how they had taken advantage of our generosity to slyly build on top of our very heads, on our property! We described how they had laughed in our faces when we confronted them, saying, "That's your problem," and 'Next time don't be so quick to do people favors." We showed everyone the *seruv* that had been publicized all over the city and repeated the many severe comments the *dayanim* had said against them at the time for the brazen chutzpah with which they behaved. We concluded with the ruling issued by the

Peace at Home

court, which proved beyond a shadow of a doubt that they were the ones in the wrong, not us.

It took me a while to realize that people simply did not believe either of us. The result was that neither our family nor theirs managed to do a single *shidduch*.

Years passed. My friends were all married but I remained single thanks to our neighbors' efforts. One day, a different neighbor, a *"gutte neshamah"* who did her best to make sure the flames of hatred between us never died down, said to my mother, "Do you know what Mrs. X's biggest fear is? That your son will marry before her daughter. She simply would not be able to bear it."

We were shocked at that comment. My parents nearly had a heart attack, but I thought about the comment and realized that my parents felt exactly the same way.

My father grew steadily more aged, shrinking into himself as the years passed. Sometimes I couldn't bear to look at his face, the tortured face of a suffering man. He rarely spoke, and when he did, his words were sharp and bitter. He became cynical and critical. He begrudged other people their good fortune.

I understood him. Watching one's children grow and develop and then be unnaturally held in check at a certain point due to the efforts of a bitter neighbor is indescribable torture.

When I was twenty-five, with three brothers and a sister behind me all waiting for *shidduchim*, warning bells began going off in my head. I realized that unless I did something about the situation, we would all remain in our parents' apartments for the rest of our lives. I tried to come up with various ideas, such as moving to a different neighborhood, but my parents made it clear that they would never consider such a step. "Besides," they said, "people would eventually know about the whole affair once they started making phone calls to check into you."

At the time, I was in contact with a young *shadchan* who had recently had great success in making matches. I had asked him to run my *shidduch* affairs. I was no longer a little boy and my parents trusted me to ask my own information and set up dates. I became quite friendly with this young man. He was my own age, married four years and the father of three children, and we hit it off very well.

Right at the outset, he understood what the problem was. "Listen here," he told me, "this is not going to just die down. They will never stop besmirching your family."

We discussed what we could do about the problem. I told him that if it were up to me, I'd return the money if only they'd stop ruining our lives. That was a very hard step for me to take, considering the hatred I'd had for them all these years, but I'd already decided that I would not carry this awful fight into another generation. I asked my friend if he would try to speak with them, but we both knew there was nothing he could really do.

One day, he called me up. "Guess who contacted me to ask if I had any *shidduch* suggestions for his children? Your next-door neighbor."

The neighbors, too, had a row of boys and girls of marriageable age. I knew the boys well from the fights we used to have ever since we were children. I asked if he would try to soften the father, to persuade him to accept the money back from us in exchange for his agreement to stop sabotaging our chances at *shidduchim*.

He tried, without success. The neighbor was every bit as tough as my father. He wouldn't hear of any attempts at appeasement. I understood that what went on in our house was more or less going on in theirs as well: They were suffering the same agony, anger and pain.

Eventually, we began sending messages to each other via the *shadchan*. It went like this: I would tell the *shadchan* to tell his wife to tell the neighbor's daughter to tell her parents in as gentle a manner as possible that perhaps we would be willing to do something about the money. Then she would get back to the *shadchan*'s wife and tell her to tell her husband to inform me that she had tried but there was nothing doing. Her father wouldn't hear of it.

The *shadchan* and his wife told me (and her, too) that we saw eye-to-eye on the matter and that if it were up to us — we would be able to put the whole matter behind us.

But it was not up to us.

We both tried to explain to our parents that unless we reached an understanding of some sort, we would both be stuck for life, but neither side would budge.

꧁ ꧁ ꧁

One day, I thought of a way to possibly soften my father's stand and have him send a messenger to speak with the neighbor. It was becoming rather tiresome to send messages through my *shadchan* friend and his wife, so when I told him about my idea, he suggested that we make a conference call so that all four of us could discuss the situation together.

The *shadchanim* arranged the call and I presented my

plan. The neighbor's daughter made some comments and the *shadchanim* added their suggestions. In the end, we decided that we would each look into the matter further and discuss the situation again a few days later.

Immediately after that conversation, I called the *shadchan* and said, "Don't even think about it." He innocently replied that he wasn't thinking about anything; he was merely trying to make the whole process more efficient. I didn't believe him, but I knew there was no chance that what he was thinking could come to fruition.

At first, our conversations were very matter-of-fact, but then they began becoming more personal. I've always had a keen intuition, and I told my parents that there was a good suggestion in the works, so they shouldn't try to suggest anything else. My parents were not surprised. At the age of twenty-five, a *bachur* is trusted to take care of his own *shidduchim*. What's more, they knew that the suggestion had been made by my *shadchan* friend, whom they knew and trusted.

My conversations with the neighbors' daughter never resulted in a peace treaty between our fathers, but eventually we reached the simple and quiet understanding that we were very compatible. Unfortunately, we also came to the even deeper and quieter understanding that we would never be able to marry due to the terrible fight.

Since we no longer had anything to discuss, we stopped communicating. My suffering now increased tenfold.

It took me two weeks to call the *shadchan* and ask him to try and "feel out" what was going on, and it took him a split second to tell me that the other side was also trying to "feel out" how I felt. I asked him to officially suggest the match — with her consent, of course.

Peace at Home

He got back to me with her consent — and a question. "She asked if you're prepared for the tumult that would result."

"Yes," I replied. "I am."

❧ ❧ ❧

World War III broke out an hour later. The *shadchan* called both my parents and hers and made the suggestion. If fury and shock were explosive materials, our building would have been blown to smithereens.

My parents came to me in shock, and hers to her. At first they were merely furious; then they threatened me; and finally, they wept. In the end, they both informed us — as if they had discussed it — that as far as they were concerned, we could marry in the street. We both informed our parents — as if we had discussed it — that that's what we intended to do.

Since both our families follow *da'as Torah*, the *shadchan* suggested to both sets of parents that they each should speak to their *rabbanim*. The crisis was over within a week — both sides gave in and agreed to allow the match to proceed.

It took another two weeks to arrange for an official engagement at which time both sides would finally meet. Many good people got involved and the engagement took place. I can't begin to describe how many tears were shed. Everyone was crying: my parents and hers, the other neighbors, and all our relatives — everyone who knew how terribly the rift between the two families had affected us.

Our families' *mazal* changed with our engagement. Within the year, two of my siblings and three of hers celebrated their engagements. By the time we got married, my *mechutanim* had already loosened up somewhat. Perhaps they finally understood what they had done to themselves all those years and how our *shidduch* had saved them from themselves.

I wrote this story to you with my wife's consent, for the benefit of readers who are embroiled in even a minor argument with a neighbor. Don't do this to yourselves. Swallow your pride and forgo your money; just don't eat your heart out.

My wife and I live in a building with eleven other families. The moment there is so much as a hint of an argument between two families, my wife and I exchange a very meaningful glance. That glance contains the entire story I just told you, and a lot more.

A Costly Simchah

Simchahs must be paid for.
  Some people can afford to make lavish simchahs while others make do with more modest ones.
  The hero of our story threw a lavish party for his son's bar mitzvah even though he couldn't afford so much as a modest one. Before you accuse him of rashness and irresponsibility, take a moment to read his story...

I learn in *kollel* and my wife works as a secretary. Naturally, we're in the lowest percentile as far as income is concerned. If you consider the fact that we rent our apartment rather than own it, you will realize that we just barely make ends meet.

Almost every day, I hear people complain that the air-conditioning in their car isn't working properly or that the renovations they're doing are coming along too slowly. I think to myself: *What are you complaining about?* I don't own a car and chances are I never will. I think twice before taking the bus anywhere. Every month, it's a struggle to keep a roof over our heads and food on the table.

I'm not sure how we manage to survive, but the fact is that with Hashem's help, we do, and our children do well in school and are well-liked by their peers.

I have two girls followed by five boys. Girls cost less than boys. With a girl, there's no *shalom zachar* and no *bris milah* to make, just the regular expense of diapers and formula. Boys, on the other hand, mean big expenses the moment they're born.

On the other hand, some balance is achieved because the gifts received at a *bris* usually cover the expenses — unless the *bris* comes out on Shabbos, in which case people forget to send a gift after Shabbos and you're left with the expenses.

I know it might sound strange to you that I'm calculating every detail of my children's lives according to income and expenses, but I calculate my every breath according to income and expenses. That's the only way I can keep my family afloat.

I've never run after money. What I'm after is peace of mind. My dreams involve a home I own free and clear, clothing and food. Maybe normal people can't understand what I'm talking about, but for me, these are the concerns that occupy my thoughts.

As I said, my third child is our first boy. When he was twelve and a half, I began discussing with my wife how we would celebrate his bar mitzvah.

Obviously, we would not have a lavish affair. Our discussion revolved around whether we'd celebrate at home or in the hall of our local shul.

My wife vetoed the idea of doing it at home. She said

A Costly Simchah

that none of his friends had celebrated their bar mitzvahs at home and he would be very upset at the idea. I pointed out that his friends hadn't celebrated their bar mitzvahs in a shul, either, so according to that reasoning, the shul also wasn't an option.

We deliberated back and forth, and finally we decided to go with a very simple hall in our neighborhood. A few members of our community had also made bar mitzvahs there. This way, our son wouldn't feel inferior to others, or at least not to everyone else.

When we told our son where we were planning to hold his bar mitzvah, his face darkened. He wasn't pleased, but he didn't say a word. I explained to him what he already knew: that we couldn't afford a fancy hall. My son asked if we'd hire a one-man band and I replied that it was unnecessary; we could bring along a CD player and some music CDs instead.

He didn't say a word. I saw that he was upset, but he dealt with it the way he dealt with similar disappointments he'd endured in his life, such as our inability to pay for swimming lessons (I taught him myself, at the beach), day camp and many other "luxuries."

Objections to the hall we'd chosen came from a surprising source: my uncle.

My uncle is a well-to-do businessman who owns a successful chain of stores.

He happened to hear where we were planning to celebrate our son's bar mitzvah, and when I met him at another bar mitzvah, he asked me directly: "Do you really intend to make a bar mitzvah that's so... unrespectable?"

"What makes a bar mitzvah respectable?" I asked him.

"Well, I don't expect you to rent the fanciest hall in town, the way I do for my *simchah*s, but take a decently decorated place with mirrors and nice lighting. Rent chair covers for a few bucks apiece; they give an affair an instant upgrade. Good food, a nice band... give your son a decent affair. This is your oldest son, isn't it?"

"Yes," I replied, "but... these things cost a fortune, you know."

"Let me tell you something," he replied. "People make all types of stingy calculations, but they don't realize that if you make a *simchah* in a pathetic hall, the guests give stingy gifts — not because they're trying to punish you, but because they realize what your standards are. It's as if you're announcing that small sums are a fortune to you, so they give you that type of 'fortune.'" If you make a *simchah* in a fancy hall, on the other hand, people are ashamed to give measly gifts, and in the end, you cover the cost of your *simchah* either way.

"But can anyone guarantee me that people will indeed give generous gifts?" I asked. "What if I'm left with nothing?"

He winked at me. "You can trust me," he said.

To me, his wink was perfectly clear: "I'll give you a present so generous, it'll all be worth your while."

I spoke to my wife and told her I was planning to upgrade to a nicer hall and also hire a band. She couldn't understand why I'd changed my mind. I told her about my conversation with my uncle, but she remained unconvinced, pointing out that whatever we did for our oldest son, we'd have to do for his younger brothers, too. I insisted, however, that if my uncle had made such an offer, it wasn't fair to the child to make him a bar mitzvah less posh than those of his friends. Besides, it would be hurtful to my uncle, who was concerned for the respectability of our family.

A Costly Simchah

We went ahead with our plans for a fancier bar mitzvah.

◆   ◆   ◆

We canceled our booking at the first hall, which involved losing our hundred-dollar deposit, and booked a nicer hall. We ordered a nice meal and hired a band. My son was on cloud nine and we hoped and prayed we had made the right decision.

The evening was truly beautiful. True, we were upset that a few of the people we had invited hadn't come. People don't always realize how important it is for the host to have them participate in his joy. But those who had come, along with my son's friends, made sure the atmosphere was very festive and joyous.

My uncle came with his entire family, including his married children and their spouses. I was very glad to see them. I remembered his wink, which to my mind had been an explicit promise to shoulder a significant part of the expense of my *simchah*.

When the evening was over, we collected the presents and opened the lock-box in which the guests deposited their gift-checks.

Considering the number of guests we'd had, there were relatively few envelopes. I was a bit anxious, because I knew this event had been a bit of a gamble. I'd relied heavily on my guests to pay for the expenses involved, at least most of them.

We arrived home. The bar-mitzvah boy immediately began opening his gifts, which were mainly *sefarim*, while my wife and I began opening the envelopes.

Most of the sums were rather paltry, but we were waiting to see how much my uncle had given. It didn't take long for us to open the envelopes, as there weren't many. When we were done, we knew two things:

1. The amount of cash in the envelopes did not cover even ten percent of the expenses we had incurred in making the *simchah*.
2. There was no envelope from my uncle.

My wife and I stared at one another in shock. I felt a chill of fear run down my spine. Some people will not be able to understand, but this is how someone feels who has to pay a sum he doesn't have.

My wife began crying softly. I asked her to go to her room so that the children wouldn't see and become alarmed. I must note that our children had never been privy to our financial difficulties. We always went to great lengths to make sure they remained completely unconcerned. True, they knew we couldn't afford all sorts of extras, but they never sensed that we were worried about covering our basic expenses. I recommend that anyone coping with financial problems do the same, because the biggest drawback of poverty is the fear and tension that so often accompanies it.

I sat in our dining room and pondered the problem. The only hope was that my uncle had forgotten to leave a check and would surely bring it over to us within the next few days.

But a few days passed and no one called or stopped by to deliver a gift. We fell into despair. We knew that we owed the hall a fortune and we didn't have even a fraction of the amount we needed.

We discussed the situation over and over again. What really annoyed us was the fact that it had been my uncle who had persuaded us to switch from the plain hall we'd originally

A Costly Simchah

booked to the fancier one. His wink had caused us to lose our deposit on the plain hall and make a commitment to pay for expenses we couldn't afford.

We were especially surprised that my uncle had brought his entire family with him, including his married children and their spouses. We couldn't understand how a person could be so hard-hearted.

My wife wanted me to discuss the situation with my siblings or my parents. At first I refused, in order not to cause them distress, but on my wife's insistence, I finally spoke to my parents. They were taken aback, but they said they had no intentions of speaking to my uncle for fear of hurting his feelings.

I understood them: my uncle helped my parents out from time to time, as they, too, never had a dollar to spare. An ill-placed comment could easily exacerbate the situation. At the same time, they expressed their anger at his behavior. That was all they did to help me.

In the meantime, a month passed, and one day, my wife asked, "What are we going to do about our debt to the hall?"

"Honestly, we just don't have the money," I replied.

"Maybe you should take a loan?" she suggested.

"From whom?"

"We've got to do something," she said.

For the rest of that day, I walked around preoccupied with how to come up with the cash I needed to pay for the hall. Finally, I decided to take action.

I took a job cleaning buildings at night at the other end of town. According to my calculations, the salary from this job would enable me to repay my debt within a couple of months.

I knew that the owner of the hall would be calling any day

now, and I'd have no choice but to tell him the truth and ask him to allow me to pay in installments. I was glad he hadn't called so far, because I knew that the moment that call came, the pressure would really be on.

Another month passed, and still he didn't call.

I kept working and saving money. In my heart, I was furious with my uncle, so I didn't make contact with him. He didn't call us either; apparently, he had the good sense to be ashamed of what he had done to us.

◣   ◣   ◣

Three months after the bar mitzvah, I felt I had enough cash to come to the hall owner with "something" in hand. My wife, who is extremely careful with money matters, had kept asking me to call, but I'd been putting off the inevitable unpleasantness.

I went down to the hall and asked to speak with the owner. I expected him to be annoyed, but he received me with a smile.

"How are you?" he asked. "Are you making another *simchah*?"

"I haven't finished yet with the first one, and you're already asking about the next one?" I asked in surprise.

"What do you mean?" he countered. "Why do you say you haven't yet finished with the first one?"

"Don't you know what I'm talking about?"

"Not at all. Do you have any complaints that were not addressed?"

"My bill," I said. "You… it seems you've forgotten, but I haven't paid you yet."

"Of course you paid," he protested. "Do I look like the type of guy who forgets a dollar that's owed to him?"

A Costly Simchah

I was shocked. "But... but I didn't pay you," I said weakly. "Did you get money from me?"

"No, I never stay until the end of a *simchah*, but my manager received payment from you."

"Can I speak with him?"

"Sure." He called his manager, who was in one of the smaller halls downstairs, and asked him to come up.

The manager came into the office.

"Do you remember me?" I asked.

"Of course. You made a bar mitzvah here," he replied. "But that's not why I remember you," he added. "Lots of people make bar mitzvahs here, after all. But a tip like you gave me — that I don't forget!"

"I gave you a tip? I didn't even pay you!"

"Of course," he said, waving his hand in dismissal. "You sent your father or someone. He paid for the *simchah* and left a fat tip for me and the waiters in your name."

I felt faint. The walls seemed to spin.

"How did he pay?" I asked.

"With a check. Why do you ask?"

"Can you check the information on the check?" I asked.

"Sure, we have it on record," the owner said. "What was the date of your *simchah*?"

I told him the date and he riffled through his receipt book. "Here's a copy of the check."

The name on the check was that of my uncle.

◄   ◄   ◄

I collapsed into a chair and began to cry.

They stared at me in shock, wondering what was going on.

"For the past three months, I've been furious at this man because he promised to give a handsome check at the bar mitzvah but never did," I explained. "I've been avoiding him and thinking all kinds of terrible thoughts about him, and now I see how wrong I've been."

They listened as I related what I had gone through over the past few months, and the hall owner said, "If you knew me better, you would know that there was no way I wouldn't have called you the day after the *simchah* and every day thereafter."

I hurried to my wife's workplace and told her the astounding news. We both felt happy and sad at the same time: happy at the good news that we were not in debt, but sad that we had wrongly suspected our generous uncle of behaving inappropriately.

"What do we do now?" my wife asked.

"We've got to go visit him, tell him the truth and thank him," I replied.

That evening, we went to visit him with a gift of appreciation and a bouquet of flowers. We sat down and told him candidly what we had endured over the past few months. Of course, we didn't tell him what we had thought and said about him, just that we were worried and very surprised.

My uncle was very moved. He told us that he, for his part, had been surprised at us for not calling. Why, he'd even felt annoyed that we hadn't acknowledged his gift. It hadn't dawned on him that we were simply unaware that he had paid the bill.

The story ended well. We made a beautiful bar mitzvah and were left with a tidy little sum from the gifts and from the money I'd saved up working to pay for the affair...

And we learned a very tangible lesson in judging our fellow man favorably.

Pictures of Life

A young woman is widowed when her husband dies of a serious illness.

A few years later, she gets remarried to a man very different in personality from her first husband, yet very special in his own right.

Their life together is off to a wonderful start... and then they chance upon a photo album...

I've been intending to write to you for a long time, but a life story like mine is rather difficult to commit to paper.

At the age of twenty, I married a kind and wonderful man. Our wedding was an event everyone remembered for a long time because it was just so perfect. Everyone present commented that we made a perfect couple, and it was true. We were a lovely, wonderful couple.

We settled in to our new home and began building our family. My husband worked as a teacher and so did I. Life was good.

Over the next eight years, three children were born to us: two girls and a boy. How happy my husband was when our first son was born after two girls! The *bris milah* was a big event. My husband was so excited that we finally had a boy to perpetuate the family name.

The trouble began shortly thereafter.

❦ ❦ ❦

My husband began complaining of pain in his chest area. At first, we thought it would pass. He took an EKG, which showed that everything was in order; but the pain persisted, so he underwent extensive testing. The resulting diagnosis changed everything: lung cancer.

Here began a terrible period in our lives: hospitalizations, radiation, chemotherapy, hair loss, nausea. At times, there seemed to be some improvement, but then the disease was back full force. My husband deteriorated in front of my very eyes, and at some point it became clear that there was nothing we could do. He asked to return home, and I did my best to care for him during the final stage of his life.

During this time, we had many serious conversations — about the children, their *chinuch*, and how he wanted them to remember him. We spoke about the future and about his pain at not seeing them grow up and marry. He spoke a lot about *parnasah*, worrying how I'd manage. He showed me where he'd put important documents. Although one's instinct at such a time is to say, "Don't talk like that; you'll get well," the bond we shared made it possible to speak openly — even about such topics. I listened to everything that was important to my husband to say so that he'd depart this world knowing he was surrounded by love and support.

Toward the end, he asked me to summon a few people from the shul and from his workplace whom he feared he might have wronged at some point. He asked their forgiveness, and although at first they protested that these were trivial incidents and there was no need to ask forgiveness, in the end they assured him that they forgave him with all their heart.

"I can't think of anyone else whom I may have hurt," he told me, "but if you think of anyone to whom I owe money or an apology, please tell me. And if I'm no longer here by then, please take care of the matter in my place."

During his final week, he spoke about his desire for the children to have a father and he asked me to remarry after he was gone. I didn't want to hear of it at that point, but he said, "Remember that I asked you to do this." These were more or less his final words. Immediately thereafter, he lost consciousness and two days later, he returned his pure soul to the Creator.

I became a widow before the age of thirty. Life hurled me into a difficult reality for which I was completely unprepared. I went through *shivah*, *shloshim*, and "the year" with three young children whom I now had to raise on my own.

I did my best to be a good, happy mother to my children despite the difficulty involved. My husband had left a sum of money that helped provide for us. At some point, I returned to work to earn a living, and somehow we survived another three very difficult years.

At this point, people began suggesting *shidduch* prospects for me. At first, I refused to listen, even feeling annoyance toward those who tried to make suggestions, but then a certain *rebbetzin* made me reconsider. "For the next week," she told me, "try to see your children objectively, and ask yourself whether you are helping or harming them by refusing to consider remarriage." She paused for a moment and then asked, "What would your husband, of blessed memory, want you to do?"

Well, I knew the answer to that. He had made himself perfectly clear to me and also written as much in his will, but I was in too much pain.

I followed the *rebbetzin*'s suggestion and observed my children for a week, at the end of which I understood that I had to make an effort to remarry. I agreed to listen to suggestions.

At first, the suggestions I received were for people very much like my husband: charismatic, self-confident movers and shakers. I met with a few of these men but didn't click with any of them. I don't know why. For some reason, they frightened me in a way that my husband, with his strong personality, never had. Perhaps the years I'd spent alone had turned me so fiercely independent that I didn't want a stranger entering my life and beginning to manage it for me.

Then someone suggested a thirty-two-year-old divorced man who was completely different from my husband. He was quieter and more refined; he had a desk job that required little contact with others. But he was honest, sincere, a pleasant conversationalist, nice-looking and refined. You couldn't have found someone more different from my late husband.

And he was the one I found suitable.

I asked around and learned that the divorce was not his fault and that he had two children whom he showered with love. I decided to accept the *shidduch*.

We married. My new husband joined my children and me at our house and we began life anew.

Baruch Hashem, I soon saw that I had made the right choice. My husband was pleasant and refined, ethical and

Pictures of Life

smart. My children got along with him beautifully, and after a while, his children began spending every other Shabbos with us.

We all adjusted to a new routine and I began healing.

We didn't speak much about my late husband or his ex-wife. I told my new husband I'd had a wonderful marriage. He, for his part, related that his first marriage been awful. We didn't dwell on the topic, though. We knew what we had to know.

Or so we thought.

One day, I told my husband I wanted to show him pictures of my childhood. I began showing him albums with photos of me as a baby, a child, and a teen. Then we looked at the photos of my first wedding.

Suddenly, I spotted an album with photos of my late husband's childhood. For some reason, I opened it and asked my husband if he wanted to look at the pictures.

"Why not?" he said.

I turned a page and suddenly, he gasped. "Oh, my goodness," he said. "Who is that?"

"This is my late husband, as a child," I replied.

I saw that he was in shock.

"What's the matter?" I asked.

"Nothing. I... I mean..."

I stared at him. His face was white.

"What's the matter?" I asked. "You look like you've seen a ghost."

"No, I... I recognized him... he... I think we knew each other as children."

"What do you mean? How did you know him?"

"Yes, it's him," I heard him murmur to himself. "How could I not have realized?"

I was alarmed. "Can you please tell me what you're talking about?"

"I don't think it would be a good idea," my husband said.

"You must tell me."

"Please, just let it go," he pleaded. "I'm afraid of what might happen if you hear the story. Just pretend I never said anything."

I knew I couldn't live with that. "Look," I said. "I don't know what might happen after I hear the story, but I know what will happen if you don't tell me."

Poor thing, a gentle soul like my husband couldn't possibly remain firm in the face of such aggressiveness. He capitulated.

◆ ◆ ◆

"Do you remember I told you that as a child, my family lived in Yerushalayim for half a year?"

"Yes," I said. My second husband had been born and raised in Beit Shemesh. At one point, his parents had moved to Yerushalayim but it hadn't worked out and they'd returned to Beit Shemesh.

"Well?" I prompted.

"I told you things hadn't worked out, but I didn't really elaborate."

"So what was the reason?"

"The truth is that for them, things worked out pretty well. We found a great apartment not far from where my father worked. It was me who didn't do well. My parents sent me to Talmud Torah _____" (he named the school my late husband had attended as a child).

"I was in fourth grade, and although to this day I don't know why, I was targeted for extreme bullying.

"First I was given a horrid nickname." He told me what it was, and it was truly humiliating. "Nobody wanted to sit near me. My stuff was stolen from my backpack. I was humiliated in front of boys from other classes. I had always been a quiet boy who made and received no trouble, but now my classmates were tormenting me beyond belief.

"At some point, my parents realized that something was the matter and they alerted the school to the problem. The teacher and the principal did their best to remedy the situation, but there was one boy, the undisputed leader of the class, who refused to allow the others to take pity on me. I will never forget that boy's face…"

My husband opened the photo album. "When I first heard your late husband's name, I didn't make the connection because it's a rather common name, and I knew him by the childish nickname by which he was called rather than the name he used as an adult. Even when I saw the photos of him as an adult, it didn't register. But I will never in a hundred years forget the face of the child who made my life miserable for six months…"

He took a deep breath and went on. "I was in that school for only a half a year because my parents realized that if I continued there, I'd suffer irreversible damage. I remember their desperate attempts to solve the problem and their despairing looks when they saw me shriveling in front of their eyes. They tried to switch me to a different school, but the other schools reacted with suspicion when they heard I was dropping out of the first school after just a few months.

"In the end, we returned to Beit Shemesh. I went back to my old class in my old school, but whoever knew me saw that I was no longer the same child. From a happy, carefree and confident child, I had become a frightened, hesitant, hypersensitive shadow of my former self."

My husband went on to relate some of the difficulties he'd suffered during the latter part of his childhood and his adolescence, and how he had managed to overcome those hindrances and build himself into who he was today.

"I tried so hard to build myself up that I forgot what had caused the change in me in the first place, but now, when I saw his photo in front of me, it all came back. I realized that I had forgotten, but not forgiven. No, that isn't right: I never really forgot, either. I just suppressed the memories."

"What do we do now?" I asked him.

"Are... are you okay with me even now that you know?" he asked apprehensively.

"Well, I do feel some unpleasantness, though I don't know why. It's as if I had a part in all this."

"You had no part in it," he said firmly. "On the contrary, you have had a part in helping me regain my sense of worth."

He began describing to me what he had endured during his first marriage to a woman who had exploited his kindness and gentleness to hurt him deeply. We both wept into the wee hours of the night at the suffering he'd endured. In my heart, I thought that the fact that he'd allowed someone to step on him like that must have some connection to what he'd gone through as a child.

He guessed what I was thinking and said, "I don't blame him for that. Even if I was lacking in self-confidence, that was no reason for her behave the way she did. For a long time, I thought something was the matter with me, but finally, someone convinced me that that wasn't the case. Do you know who it was?"

He paused and then went on. "It was you. You restored the self-confidence I lacked. With your kindness, your fairness, your good heart and wonderful *middos*, you proved to me that it wasn't me who was problematic. As an *eishes chayil*, you awakened the personality lying dormant within me and gave me the confidence to rebuild the self-esteem every person needs to function at his best. Isn't it fascinating how Hashem arranged it that out of all the people in this world, I found happiness with you — the widow of the man who started it all?"

We were silent for a moment and then he said, "Now what will be with him?"

"Yes?" I asked, afraid to voice what I was thinking.

"You probably want me to forgive him, don't you?"

I nodded and related that before his passing, my late husband had appointed me his messenger to ask *mechilah* from anyone who I learned he'd hurt in any way.

"Did he really ask you that?" he asked in surprise.

"Yes, he did. I suppose it was a prophetic statement on his part."

"Well, then, you've fulfilled your mission. Tomorrow we'll go to his *kever* together, you and I, and I will forgive him with all my heart for what happened when we were children."

We went to sleep for about an hour. Then we woke the children, sent them off to school and drove to the cemetery.

I didn't go to the *kever* because the custom is that a woman who has remarried does not visit the grave of her first husband, but my husband stood there for a long while. Then he returned to where I was standing, and I saw that his gait was much more confident than before.

"I forgave him and also myself for all the things for which I'd blamed myself throughout the years," he said.

◆ ◆ ◆

We got into the car, and just as my husband was about to drive off, I said, "I have something to show you."

He waited.

Before leaving for the cemetery, I'd quickly gone through the album where we'd found the bombshell the previous night. I'd had a feeling I'd find what I was looking for, and indeed I had.

"Tell me, in the half year you were in Yerushalayim, did you go on a class trip?"

"I think so... I think we went to Haifa for a boat ride."

"You're right. It occurred to me that in the half a year you were there, you might have landed up in a photo with my late husband — and I was right."

I withdrew from my purse a faded picture in which my late husband, z"l, is standing side-by-side with my second husband. Incredibly enough, in the photo they looked as if they were the best of friends.

Photographs, apparently, sometimes lie, but life... now, that's an altogether different story.

The Reward for a Kabbalah

Every girls high school has a list of rules and regulations its students are expected to obey.

Most girls do, but there are always some who try to circumvent the rules or even openly flaunt them.

This story, told by a mechaneches, is about a student who found it difficult to abide by the rules, yet agreed to change her attitude and behavior completely from one moment to the next — on one condition...

I'm a *mechaneches* in a well-known high school. I deliberated long and hard over whether to write this story, but I felt that in the end, the potential benefits outweighed the possible risks.

A girl from a very simple family attended our high school. There had been some deliberation over whether or not to accept her because of her family background, but in the end, her good marks and fine character stood in her good stead.

Before you get upset, allow me to explain my intention when I say "a simple family." I am not referring to people lacking money or status. It's no secret that the first girls to be accepted to our school are the daughters of *avreichim*, most of whom do not have money and do not hold important positions.

In our jargon, "simple" refers to family with weak *hashkafos*, where the parents fail to instill in their children a love for Torah or impress upon them the obligation to obey *talmidei chachamim*. They might be wealthy and aristocratic, but as far as the high school is concerned, they're "simple people." Their children are liable to have difficulty conforming to the exacting school rules and might even act as a negative influence on other girls.

Before I begin my story, I would like to say something on behalf of all the *chareidi* high schools that are so often attacked by "*chareidi*" websites and media outlets and also by ordinary people.

Wherever you go you can hear people grumble, "Why don't they accept everyone who applies to their high school?" or "Why do they act as if the thickness of the stockings the girls wear is the most important thing on earth?" Comments like these are made with anger, scorn, or even hatred, but the obvious question is: Why do people want to send their children to these schools, even fighting to get in? How do you explain the paradox: parents will do anything to get their daughter into a certain school and then turn around and attempt to undermine its rules?

After giving much thought to the matter. I've reached two conclusions: First, when parents choose a high school for their daughters, they give priority to the name the school has and the status it will give them. They're more concerned for *shidduchim* than for finding the right fit for their daughter. Second, people don't understand that there's an inherent

The Reward for a Kabbalah

connection between a school's strictness in *tznius* matters and its good name.

❦ ❦ ❦

Some parents complain: "What's wrong with wearing a skirt so long it brushes the floor? Why, it's even more modest than a knee-length skirt!"

Most of the time, people who make such arguments are merely pretending to be obtuse. Everyone understands that there's more to modesty than covering certain areas; it's also unbecoming to dress in an overly casual "streetlike" manner. A *chareidi* man, for example, will not walk around in a baseball cap, even though, technically speaking, the cap covers more of his head than a *yarmulke*.

If the person voicing such questions honestly does not understand, the situation is no less problematic, because it means that he or she just doesn't "get" *chareidi* norms — and norms are incredibly important in the *chareidi* world. If you don't understand them, you aren't ready to be integrated in a *chareidi* framework.

With boys, too, arguments of this type stem either from naiveté or false naiveté: What's wrong with cotton pants? So what if my belt buckle is as large as the sunglasses people wear nowadays?

In most cases, the people voicing these complaints will, in a moment of sincerity, admit that they really do very well understand what the problem is.

If I sound like a high school teacher, it's because, as I've already pointed out, I am one.

❦ ❦ ❦

Now for the story.

The girl, as I said, came from a simple family; that is, financially stable but spiritually weak. The father hadn't attended yeshivah as a boy, nor had the mother received her education in a Beis Yaakov school. Their attitude toward *chareidi* educational institutions was decidedly hostile.

Still, the girl was a top student and very refined in her behavior. The management decided to accept her in the hope that the school would inculcate her with proper *hashkafos*.

But that hope did not materialize. The girl was not disrespectful to her teachers, nor did she introduce problematic *hashkafos*, but her manner of dress most definitely did not conform to school regulations. There's no point in going into detail; suffice it to say that in all areas of *tznius*, she walked a fine line between that which is acceptable and that which is not — sometimes crossing that line completely.

We spoke with her about these issues on numerous occasions, and when that didn't work we contacted her parents.

Parents who receive such messages usually react in one of three ways:

1. Some parents accept the remarks with due seriousness and immediately work to effect a change.
2. Some parents behave hypocritically. They pretend to accept what the school is saying and promise to make an immediate change. They'll tell their daughter to follow the rules, but won't hesitate to mock the school's standards. This, of course, gives the student all the backing she's looking for with regard to her inappropriate dress or behavior, and against the school and its method of *chinuch*.
3. Some parents begin openly battling the school, arguing with the rules, pretending not to understand them

The Reward for a Kabbalah

(or really failing to understand) and continuing to allow their daughter to dress as she pleases. In such cases, it's usually only a matter of time before the student in question finds herself out of the school, either by choice or because the administration expelled her.

The parents of the girl in this story belonged to the second group. Her parents asked her to change the way she dressed, but at the same time, they spoke about how they couldn't understand the school's "fanatical" requirements. The result was that the girl continued dressing as she pleased, taking advantage of her parents' tacit support to grow increasingly bold and defy the rules to an even greater degree.

🖃 🖃 🖃

There was one *mechaneches* who always defended her, insisting that she had a certain inner purity and lofty spiritual aspirations, but none of the teachers could point to any evidence of such aspirations. In light of the situation, it was clear that it was only a matter of time until she'd be expelled.

One day, an esteemed *rebbetzin* came to address the girls on the topic of *tznius*.

Among other things, the *rebbetzin* said that when someone takes on an important *kabbalah* that involves forgoing something dear to him, *Hakadosh Baruch Hu* fulfills that person's dearest aspiration in life.

Of course, it sounded a lot more powerful when the *rebbetzin* said it, but that was the gist of her talk.

After the talk, the girl approached her *mechaneches* with a question: If she would make a resolution to forgo her preference in clothing and conform to the strict standards of the school, would she merit the materialization of her aspirations?

"What are your aspirations?" the teacher asked.

"I want to marry a true *ben Torah*, but I'm afraid that the reputation I've made for myself will ruin my chances. I'm asking if it's not too late for such a *kabbalah*."

The *mechaneches* thought a bit and said, "I'm prepared to guarantee you that you will be able to marry a true *ben Torah*. Your reputation will not harm you."

The girl then made an extreme change in her lifestyle and began obeying the regulations to the letter. At the time, we heard that her mother objected to the change (I'm always shocked at just how foolish parents can be), but she was determined to follow through on her *kabbalah*.

※ ※ ※

When the time came for *shidduchim*, she found she had a problem, albeit not from the direction she had feared. There were excellent *bachurim* who agreed, on principle, to meet her, but matters fell through because of money. Her father refused — perhaps he really was unable — to shoulder the majority of the expenses of a wedding and the costs of setting the young couple up in their own apartment; he insisted that they to go fifty-fifty. The fact of the matter is, however, that top boys expect more. (I'm sure many of your readers will be highly disapproving, but that's the way it is.)

At one point, a truly distinguished *shidduch* was suggested. The *bachur* was the top student in an elite yeshivah. The girl truly wanted this *shidduch*, but it ground to a halt because of the money issue, and she was completely broken.

She approached her *mechaneches* and said, somewhat bitterly, "You assured me that if I took upon myself to obey the school rules, even though that meant giving up something very important to me, I'd achieve my aspirations. I did it, but I can't seem to achieve what I want in life."

The Reward for a Kabbalah

The *mechaneches* thought the matter over. At first, she wanted to reassure her student that it wasn't too late and she'd yet receive a good *shidduch*, but even to her own ears, that sounded evasive.

Instead, she asked, "What's the gap between what your father can pay and what the boy's parents are asking?"

"Fifty thousand dollars," the girl replied.

"Consider it done," the *mechaneches* said without another thought. "I'm taking it upon myself to come up with the money."

The *shidduch* went back on track. Soon the couple was engaged and slowly but surely, all the teachers learned what the *mechaneches* had done. How did it come to light? Well, she began making inquiries as to how and where she might come up with the money.

None of us could understand how she could have been so irresponsible. She herself had children to marry off; how could she have undertaken a commitment of that size for someone else?

A few weeks passed and she managed to scrape together just a thousand dollars. She began to feel very pressured, but when she tried to solicit funds, people turned down her requests for assistance.

The wedding was drawing closer and she had no idea how she'd get the money.

A week before the wedding, a public activist from abroad called to ask for information about a girl from the school who had been suggested for his son. He often called her to help "pick" the best girls for his sons and relatives, and he relied heavily on her opinion.

At the end of their conversation, she asked him if he knew anyone who would consider making a sizeable contribution for *hachnasas kallah*. She told him the whole story. "I've turned to dozens of wealthy people, but I still don't have even a few thousand dollars and I promised a much larger sum."

He listened attentively and then said, "Half an hour ago, I received the will of a wealthy widow from our community who recently passed away. I haven't yet read the will, but there was a note attached to the effect that the woman had asked to bequeath a certain sum to a *kallah* who is especially careful about *tznius*, with the stipulation that the *kallah* recite a chapter of *Tehillim* in memory of her soul under the *chuppah*. I think your case fits the bill."

"How much money are we talking about?"

"It doesn't say in the note. Give me a moment to check the will. I hope it will be at least a few thousand dollars to help get you off to a good start."

She waited while he opened the envelope and read the will. Then she heard him cry out, "I don't believe it! She donated fifty thousand dollars to this cause! It can't be a coincidence. Stop collecting money. You'll have the money within a few days."

The wedding was a very joyous affair.

The *chasan* bedecked the *kallah* and a few moments later, we all accompanied her to the *chuppah*. Just before the *chasan* placed the ring on her finger, there was a moment of silence. Only those standing very close to the *chuppah* saw the *kallah* and her mother reciting a chapter of *Tehillim* with great fervor. We teachers, too, joined in and said *Tehillim* in memory of the righteous woman.

The Reward for a Kabbalah

At the wedding, *yeshivah bachurim* danced on one side of the *mechitzah* while the *kallah* danced with her family, friends and teachers on the other. Only a handful of them knew the real story behind the wedding.

If this story will inspire anyone to take on a *kabbalah* in *tznius*, it will have been worth writing.

Building Number Eighteen

A fellow who purchased a new and expensive apartment has a hard time selling his old one. He had counted on the money from the sale of the old apartment to help pay for the new one.

A few months pass and the financial pressure mounts. If that weren't enough, his job requires him to manage a huge project that takes up all his time and causes him endless aggravation.

That project is connected to this book, and the connection between the two brings him to the home of Rav Chaim Kanievsky, shlita.

What happens next is completely unexpected.

I live in Rishon Letzion. I'm married and the father of three children. I married my wife approximately twenty years ago, and with Hashem's help, we managed to build ourselves up over the years.

From a minor distributor for a well-known company, I became a branch manager, then a regional manager, and from there I was promoted to one of the senior managerial

Building Number Eighteen

positions in the company. With my new status came an improvement in my financial situation and ten years and three children later, it was time to move to a different apartment.

We looked around for awhile until we found a nice apartment in Rishon Letzion. It was far more expensive than the apartment we were living in, but since we had some savings, we decided to sell our apartment, add our savings and take a mortgage to cover the rest.

We signed a contract on the new apartment and all that was left to do was sell our old apartment.

We placed ads in the papers, but the response was poor. A few people did come to see our apartment, but no one expressed an interest in purchasing it.

After about a month of running ads in the paper, my wife suggested that I approach a real-estate agent.

I had never used a real-estate agent before because I was opposed to the concept on principle. If you can advertise in the paper to bring potential customers to your doorstep, why involve an additional party?

I held out for another month and then reluctantly gave in. I was still against real-estate agents, but I had to admit I needed help selling the apartment. I picked up the phone and began calling agents.

　　　　　🏠　　　🏠　　　🏠

I learned that being a real-estate agent is not all about making easy money. It's hard, painstaking work involving countless phone calls, incessant running around, climbing stairs and talking endessly until your voice becomes hoarse — trying to convince sellers to lower their price or to persuade buyers that they're getting a great deal.

Just like *shadchanim*, real-estate agents often experience

disappointment. For every dozen matches you attempt, only one actually comes to fruition. Even when you succeed, sometimes one party or both will attempt to deny your part in the deal and refuse you the commission they owe.

The agents who came to see my apartment told me immediately that my asking price was significantly higher than the market price. They suggested I invest in fixing it up because it looked unappealing.

They pointed to the bathroom, which had seen better days, and to the ceiling, which had cracks in it even when we moved in. The agents explained that the sorry state of our apartment, coupled with our high asking price, chased potential buyers away.

We looked into how much the renovations would cost. The cheapest guy was asking a sum we couldn't afford. We had invested all our savings in the new apartment, even taking loans. We simply could not afford to invest money in renovations, especially considering the fact that we'd never even enjoy them. Also, the agents couldn't guarantee we'd sell the apartment after fixing it up. In fact, they practically guaranteed us the opposite: No way would we sell it for the price we wanted.

A few more months passed and the owner of the apartment we had bought began pressuring us. For the first time in my life, I was under real pressure. I was anxious all day and unable to sleep at night. I'd purchased a new apartment on the assumption that I could afford it after selling my old apartment, but I'd never anticipated such a complication.

Agents came and went and slowly gave up on our apartment. That's another similarity between agents and *shadchanim*: when a case is tough, they give up and stop trying. And when they stop trying — what hope is there?

One day, the company I work for decided to conduct a special sales promotion for the *chareidi* community.

Nowadays, there are sales promotions all the time, but at the time, we conducted such promotions only once every year or two.

The special went like this: Every customer who purchased ten dollars' worth of our company's products would be eligible to purchase a book for just ten dollars.

My first reaction was: What kind of special is it that when you buy something, you become entitled to spend more money? "This is what the management decided," I was told. "You just make sure there's a steady supply of books and posters about the special displayed in all branches of the participating supermarkets. Your job is to ensure that the promotion runs smoothly."

The advertising company sent us the posters, and I made sure all the supermarkets were plastered with them. I didn't even look at the title of the book. It didn't interest me. My job was purely technical.

Some 50,000 copies of the book were sent to our offices. It was my job to deliver them to all the sales points.

Suddenly, I was informed that the special would be taking place not only at the large supermarkets but also at local groceries. That changed everything! A regular line of merchandise is one thing: the merchants know what they want and our company's sales agents take down their orders. All I had to do was supervise and make sure that merchandise was delivered as needed.

In this case, I had to make sure our sales agents explained the promotion to store owners. It had to be clear that the book was not to be sold independently of our company's products, that this special should not be combined with any other offer. We wanted them to clearly explain to customers what they needed to do to be eligible to receive — excuse me, *buy* — the book for ten bucks.

I ran from one grocery to another, explaining, arguing and sweating, while in the background, don't forget, I had my own personal problems. Every day, I fielded phone calls from the bank, the seller of the apartment we had signed for, the lawyer, and my wife who was upset to be receiving such phone calls.

And here I was, stuck running from store to store to make sure the promotion was running smoothly.

🎬 🎬 🎬

After a week of chaos, we suddenly realized what the promotion had accomplished.

Sales had simply skyrocketed. We had never sold so much merchandise during our previous marketing campaigns. Grocery stores that we'd never even heard of were ordering like supermarkets; supermarkets were ordering like retail chains; and the retail chains? We couldn't supply them with merchandise fast enough…

The company managers walked around drunk with triumph, and, of course, they praised me for the success of the campaign. But after the compliments, my workload was increased twofold.

Many branches of the retail chains complained that their supply of books had run out. They had lines of people waiting to buy more products in order to receive the privilege of buying the book at half price. I personally pleaded with and threatened the managers of the retail chains, who had warehouses full of extra books, to give some to the privately-owned groceries (the books were ours, not theirs) but they were reluctant because they wanted to make sure *they* wouldn't run out.

My daily schedule became insane. I had no time to even think about the fact that the contract I had signed on the new apartment would be declared null and void if I failed to make a payment. If that happened, I'd have to pay a huge termination fee and be stuck with the cramped and un-renovated apartment I'd come to hate.

◈ ◈ ◈

One day, I learned that our supply of books would likely be gone within the week. I called the *chareidi* advertising company that was managing the campaign and asked them to arrange to have more books printed. At the end of the week, twenty thousand copies of the book were shipped to the company. For some reason, however, the advertising company had failed to coordinate the shipment with our management and the trucks were not permitted entry to the company premises.

I received a number of angry phone calls. It was Thursday night and I was forced to leave my house and travel to the company to personally open the gates for the trucks so that the books could be delivered.

As the drivers were unloading the boxes of books, one of them fell and a couple of books fell out.

I glanced at one of the books. The title was familiar; it was the same as the name of our campaign. I checked to see the name of the author.

At this point, I hated the book for the headache it was causing me, and I hated the fellow who wrote it even more!

I'd never heard of you before. I wasn't religious; I was "traditional." *Kidspeak* was not the type of book my children read and "our heroes" were football players, not the heroes of your book…

And then, late at night, you called me, listened attentively to my barrage of complaints and then asked to meet with me in order to prepare for the next week of the campaign.

We made up to meet the following day. We met in the company offices, which were then located in the industrial area of Bnei Brak. You came with a pile of books and inscribed some dedications. You were so nice that I felt bad being angry with you. You said that if there was anything you could do to help me, it would be your pleasure.

I don't know what came over me. I immediately thought of my personal crisis and said to myself, *Here's a religious fellow. Maybe he can help from a different direction.*

"I have a certain problem," I told you. "I need a blessing from a great rabbi."

You then suggested that I come with you to Rav Chaim Kanievsky, *shlita*.

I'd heard of Rav Kanievsky before. Someone had told me that he received visitors until midnight every evening and that it was difficult to get in.

The next day, you told me to come at five, and you got me through the back door even before the official reception hours.

I recall how I was gripped by awe and fear, especially when one of the attendants gave me the honor of sitting in the chair of the Steipler, Rav Chaim's father. I recited *Tehillim* until I was told to enter the *rav*'s room.

I told him that I couldn't sell my apartment and that I was in a terrible predicament.

Building Number Eighteen

"I give you my blessing that you should sell the apartment quickly and at a good price," he said. "Just give *tzedakah*."

I withdrew my wallet and asked the *rav* how much I should give. The *rav*'s attendant said that the *rav* didn't take money for his blessings and that his intention was that I should contribute to the poor.

"Give *chai* (the alphabetic equivalent of eighteen) shekels to Kupat Ha'ir (the charity fund run by the local municipality)," Rav Chaim said. Then our meeting was over.

I left and inquired how I might contribute to Kupat Ha'ir. I contributed eighteen shekels to fulfill the *rav*'s instructions, and then I contributed an additional 180 shekels just because I wanted to.

A week passed.

One day, I received a phone call from a real-estate agent who had brought a potential customer to my apartment three months earlier.

"Ezra, do you remember me?" he asked.

"Not really," I admitted. "I've dealt with so many agents…"

"No matter," he said. "Your apartment is as good as sold."

"Sold? You were here three months ago. What made the buyer suddenly change his mind?"

"The buyer is not the one who saw your apartment. Come to my office; I have some papers for you to sign."

I didn't understand what was going on. "How does a person buy an apartment without even seeing it?"

"Ezra, it's a miracle," he said. "Come on down and I'll tell you about it."

I went quickly to his office. He told me about an Israeli fellow, a resident of Rishon Letzion, who had moved abroad and lived there for a few years. At some point, he was badly hurt in an accident that nearly cost him his life. He was miraculously spared but sustained a severe handicap. After being discharged from the hospital, he returned to Eretz Yisrael.

"He went to see a *mekubal*, who told him that he should live in Jerusalem or Tzefas. The fellow told the *mekubal* that his entire family lived in the western part of Rishon Letzion and he had no one in Jerusalem or Tzefas.

"The *mekubal* told him that he could go live in Rishon Letzion, but that he should find an apartment in a building numbered eighteen, the numerical equivalent of *chai*, as he had been spared from death.

"The man came here a week and a half ago, and since then, all the real-estate agents in the city have been searching for an apartment in a building numbered eighteen, and although it would seem that eighteen is a lucky number, no one succeeded in finding an apartment for this fellow. Every street only has one building numbered eighteen, and in the dozens of streets in Rishon Letzion, no one in number eighteen wants to sell his apartment. Who knows, maybe they also think it's a lucky number…"

I decided to look through an old list of mine, with apartments I'd long ago given up on. And on that list, lo and behold, I saw your apartment, in building number eighteen.

The buyer came to the agent's office. I asked him if he wanted to see the apartment, and he said all he needed was the plans.

"But the ceiling needs fixing up," I said.

"Alright, so I'll fix it up," he replied. "I want to close the deal."

"Okay," I said. "Let's close the deal."

Building Number Eighteen

"How do I know you won't change your mind?" he asked.

"I don't know. What do you have in mind?"

"I want to transfer the entire sum you're asking to your account right now, as per the memorandum of understanding we'll sign with the attorney," he suggested.

I looked at the agent, whose facial expression said clearly. "If you utter another word now..." So all I said was, "Uh, okay, fine with me."

Within hours, the buyer transferred the entire sum to my account. A huge stone rolled off my heart. The next day, I forwarded the money to the seller of our new apartment, which was already vacant, and two weeks later we moved.

In the course of those two weeks, the head of my company's logistics department called me and said, "Listen, we would like to extend the promotional campaign for another two weeks, but I said we could only do that with your agreement. I know how hard you worked for this campaign, and you're busy with your move and all. I'll understand if you object."

"I'll be more than happy for you to extend the campaign," I told her. "Only good came of it."

There was a long pause. "Uh, are you alright?" she asked. "Are you sure?"

"I'm sure," I reassured her.

The campaign was extended by an additional two weeks.

I'm still working in the same company and have since received a promotion. The only connection I maintained with you is that I go in to Rav Kanievsky from time to time, usually on behalf of others rather than myself. Today, a decade after that campaign, I felt the time had come to publicize this story.

The Power of Prayer

A righteous woman adopts the custom of collecting names of sick people and praying for them.

After a few years of sticking to this custom, her husband points out the possibility that many of the people she prays for have already departed this world.

Still, she continues with her custom, though her family teasingly refers to her notebook of names as the "Sick People and Yizkor Notebook."

She guards her notebook carefully, and one day everyone sees that it's the book that protects her...

My story is truly amazing. Whoever hears it tells me that it would be a mitzvah to publicize it.

My mother is an exceptionally righteous woman whose entire life has been filled with *chesed* for others. I've never heard her utter a word of *lashon hara*; she's truly an angel of pure goodness.

My parents have already married off all their children. They now have dozens of grandchildren and also a number

The Power of Prayer

of great-grandchildren. *Baruch Hashem*, they are at the stage in life where they are reaping lots of *nachas*.

About fifteen years ago, my mother spotted an ad in one of the *chareidi* newspapers which read "Please pray on behalf a woman in critical condition."

My mother wrote down the name in a little spiral notebook and began mentioning the woman's name in her prayers.

Since then, every time she saw a name in the paper or on a notice in the street, or even if she just heard about a sick person from a friend or an acquaintance, she'd jot down the name and add it to her prayers.

When I say "prayers," I'm referring to her daily "regimen" of *tefillah*, *Tehillim* and *Perek Shirah*. Within a few years, the notebook contained hundreds of names, all of which she would read at every *tefillah*. The recitation of the names considerably increased the time spent on each *tefillah*.

My father used to grumble good-naturedly about this custom, saying that he never found time to talk to her because she was always busy with her "Sick People Notebook."

Still, he served as her "main supplier" of names, because her only source was the daily paper they subscribed to, but my father was able to bring her more names from other papers and shul bulletin boards. That's my father. He might pretend to be annoyed at something, but when my mother wants something, he'll run to the ends of the earth to get it for her.

🕊 🕊 🕊

One Shabbos, at the *seudah*, my father suddenly commented that there was a good chance that a considerable number of the people she was praying for were no longer among the living.

"You shouldn't say such things!" my mother objected.

There was a moment of silence as everyone at the table considered my father's comment. Then we all said, "He's right. Some of those names were elderly people fifteen years ago. Some of them have certainly passed on by now, and she's still saying *Tehillim* for them…"

My mother's eyes filled with tears. "You think they passed away?" she said, her voice trembling slightly.

It was such a touching moment. My mother is no youngster herself, yet it had never occurred to her that the people whose welfare she was praying for might already be in a better world…

"But so what?" my mother said after a few moments of silence. "I don't think it can hurt if I *daven* for them. Even in *Shamayim*, it can only do them good if I *daven* for them."

We all burst out laughing as if it were a good joke. My mother almost felt hurt, but we kissed her and embraced her with boundless love. You have to admit that you can't help but love such a sweet, ingenuous woman.

You'd be surprised, but from that day on, we were all on the lookout for names to bring her for her "Sick People Notebook," which my father soon renamed the "Sick People and Yizkor List" over my mother's weak attempts at protest. The truth is that my mother's protests were just for show. All in all, she was glad that the notebook was occupying the minds and hearts of her loved ones.

One evening, my mother suffered a stroke. She was rushed to the hospital, where the doctors said her chances of survival were slim.

The news spread quickly through our family. Some of us

The Power of Prayer

went to the hospital while others ran to *rabbanim* to ask for a *berachah*.

We called the paper to ask them to print a notice asking people to pray for her. Having done that, we suddenly realized that now no one would be praying for all the sick and deceased people listed in our mother's notebook. We decided to do it in her place, as a merit for a *refuah sheleimah*.

My father was so miserable. A dynamic, happy person by nature, his face was now pale and pinched. He was extremely attached to my mother. He always said that he couldn't manage without her for a moment, and it was now obvious that this was no exaggeration. He ceased functioning normally; he walked around in a haze of anguished bewilderment.

The following day, her situation deteriorated and a few of my married nephews decided to hold an *erev tefillah* (evening of prayer) for her recovery. They hung signs in the neighborhood and chose a local shul as the venue.

That day, all of us sisters spent the day at the hospital, sitting in the waiting room of the intensive-care unit and praying. We discovered that the undertaking of reading all the names of the sick and deceased people on our mother's list was even greater than we had thought. We had to divide the list among the three of us, and even so, it took us far longer to *daven* than usual. Of course, each of us added our mother's name to the list of *cholim*.

The *tefillah* gathering was called for 8:00 P.M.

At 8:05, the doctors came out to tell us that our mother was on the brink of death.

They allowed us to enter her room. She was hooked up to a respirator, and there were so many machines that it was almost impossible to see her. We watched as the line showing her heartbeat slowed and then became completely flat.

Our mother returned her soul to her Creator.

⌖ ⌖ ⌖

For the next ten minutes, we wept bitterly, and then my sister said, "We need to let people know that they should stop praying."

She picked up the cell phone and called her son, who had organized the prayer gathering. Before she could finish dialing, I snatched the cell phone from her hand and closed it.

"Let them *daven*," I said. "Ima deserves to have them *daven* for her after her passing, just as she *davened* for the thousands of people on her list."

My sister objected, but my other sister agreed with me. "She's right," she declared emphatically. "If there's anyone in the world who deserves to have the *tzibbur daven* for her after her passing, it's Ima, who *davened* for an entire *tzibbur* every single day without knowing whether the people were even alive anymore.

A quarter of an hour later, the cell phone rang. The number on the screen indicated that it was my nephew.

Once again, I snatched the phone from my sister and answered the call.

My nephew inquired what the situation was.

"Nothing's changed," I told him, which was halfway true.

"There's a large crowd of people here *davening* for Savta," he said. "Let's hope Hashem will help."

"Excellent," I told him. "Keep *davening*. She deserves your *tefillos*."

"I want you to hear the *davening*," he told me.

I put the phone on speaker. My nephew entered the shul and we heard the *tzibbur* crying out, "*Kel na, refa na lah.*"

The Power of Prayer

The three of us burst into uncontrollable tears. We knew all too well that it was too late for that.

At this point, my conscience began troubling me. I don't know whether my sisters felt the same way, but I felt like we were lying to an entire *tzibbur*. I decided that when my nephew put the phone back to his ear, I'd tell him that he could stop the *tefillah* because his grandmother was no longer alive.

But my nephew was immersed in prayer and the cell phone was on his *shtender*. I heard him cry out together with the rest of *tzibbur*: "*Maskil leDavid behiyoso... koli el Hashem ezak...eshpoch lefanav...tzarasi lefanav agid.*"

The roar of *Tehillim* soared Heavenward and I was about to hang up and call again.

Just then, we noticed lots of activity going on around us. Doctors and nurses with resuscitation equipment were running to our mother's room. I entered and saw her bed surrounded by doctors.

I glanced at the screen and miraculously enough, there was some activity. It was faint but unmistakable. The doctors began resuscitating her and we were shooed out of the room. We joined those praying in the shul with prayers of our own, weeping and crying out to Hashem, oblivious to what was going on around us.

After a few long moments, a doctor stepped out. He told us that a miracle had transpired. One of the nurses had suddenly noticed a slight movement. Our mother was showing signs of life. "She's now stable," he said. "Her condition is still serious, but her life does not appear to be in danger anymore."

Our mother survived her stroke, returned home, and after

months of intensive rehabilitation, she's walking, talking and functioning in a manner befitting a woman of her age. She has to take medication, but other than that, everything is fine.

We no longer laugh at her list of sick and deceased people. We are well aware that the thousands of people for whom our mother prayed after their demise went to the *Kisei Hakavod* and pleaded with Hashem to grant her additional years of life. Joining them were those in this world who had no idea that she was already gone.

I think the lesson of this story is obvious. I would like to add, though, that my mother is no longer the only one in our family to keep a list of sick and deceased people. All her daughters now follow her example, and perhaps, after reading this story, many other people will join us, as well.

The Only Thing to Fear Is Fear Itself

This is a special story about the righteous Rebbetzin Batsheva Kanievsky, a"h.

Much has been written about the warmth and love she radiated to Jewish women and the kind words she showered upon everyone who came to see her.

The heroine of this story had the merit of having Rebbetzin Kanievsky speak with her harshly.

When you read this story, you will understand why she can't stop thanking her to this day...

I've been keeping my story in my heart for many years, but the sudden passing of Rebbetzin Batsheva Kanievsky, a"h, wife of Rav Chaim Kanievsky, *yibadel lechaim tovim*, prompted me to share it with the public.

Like everyone else, I read the many marvelous stories about her that appeared in various periodicals. These stories discussed her boundless love for her Jewish sisters, the open miracles that transpired with her involvement, and the blessings she gave that came true.

The most striking aspect of her personality, however, was the maternal warmth she radiated to everyone she met.

As one who visited the Rebbetzin numerous times, I can testify that every Jewish woman — even those who were completely estranged from *Yiddishkeit* — was treated with the strongest warmth and love imaginable. Women consulted with her about matters that would make most *chareidi* woman cringe, but she just embraced them and showered them with compliments and warm words: "You're a *tzadekes*." "You have a beautiful *neshamah*." "You're wonderful." Amazingly enough, these women always left feeling spiritually strengthened simply by virtue of the fact that they were received without a hint of criticism.

And that's why I think my story is unique. I think I'm the only one at whom the Rebbetzin was once truly angry. I might be exaggerating; maybe she wasn't really angry — but she spoke with me very sharply, the way she never spoke with anyone else. And her anger was the greatest act of *chesed* ever done to me, and I believe one of the greatest acts of *chesed* she ever committed — which is saying a lot.

I married at the age of eighteen.

Two years after my wedding, I gave birth to a son. Understandably, I was overjoyed. We made a *bris* and then a *pidyon haben*.

A year and a half later, I was expecting again, but there were complications. I sensed that something was terribly wrong. We went to a top doctor, who told me that he could operate, but that the surgery posed a risk to my life.

A few days passed and I was hospitalized.

When I was discharged, I knew that I would not be giving

The Only Thing to Fear Is Fear Itself

birth to my second child within the next few months.

I struggled with and eventually came to terms with my loss. The trouble was that the words the doctor had told me about life-threatening surgery would not leave me. I could not get them out of my mind. Long after I had healed physically from the trauma of what I had been through, I bore emotional scars that refused to heal.

I was terrified to become expecting again. Whenever I thought about it, I was gripped by a sense of impending doom.

My husband sent me to the *rebbetzin* while he went to see *rabbanim*. They sent me to doctors and psychologists, all of whom said the same thing: I had no medical problem. My mind was sending a message to my body, warning it not to get pregnant.

I knew they were right. I didn't want to bear another child. The words "life-threatening surgery" hounded me relentlessly.

My poor husband knew that I was afraid of bearing more children, and the situation frustrated him to no end. He pleaded with me to want a larger family, but I would tell him, "I'm afraid to want. I'm afraid I'll need surgery. I have terrible anxiety. I just can't."

I pitied him, but my fear for my own wellbeing overpowered my pity. On top of my fear, I now felt guilty. Both my husband and I were miserable about the situation.

This went on for eight and a half years.

Throughout those years, I went to Rebbetzin Kanievsky a number of times. I told her what I had been through and that I was terribly frightened. Each time, she embraced me and blessed me that my fears should disappear.

But it didn't help. My fears remained firmly in place.

In my mind, the Rebbetzin's kindly embraces served as confirmation that my fears were justified.

Years passed. My husband suffered bouts of depression. He couldn't bear to see the best part of our lives passing us by. His siblings' and friends' families were expanding while ours remained small.

◆ ◆ ◆

One day, my husband and I went to Rav Kanievsky's house. By Divine Providence, only the Rebbetzin was home, and she received us graciously.

My husband poured out his heart to her, weeping bitterly. He told her how anguished he was that his wife couldn't get a grip on her fears.

She asked questions that made it clear this was the first time she was grasping the full complexity of the situation.

"You mean there's no physical problem?" she asked. "Is that what the doctors say? It's all psychological? Are you sure?"

When my husband assured her that this was the case, the smile faded from her face and her demeanor turned very serious. "I want to discuss this with my husband," she told me. "Come back tomorrow on your own."

I returned the following day, unsure whether to be hopeful or afraid.

She took me into a room and there I faced a Rebbetzin Kanievsky that I had never known and that I don't think anyone else has ever seen.

She began praising my husband, who wanted children so badly but had for years suffered in silence so as to avoid pressuring me. Then she said, "What can you tell a woman who is scared? That she shouldn't be scared? It sounds so unfeeling, so insensitive. It's impossible to be angry at a woman because she's scared. She needs support; she needs to be listened to attentively and soothed that it's okay to be frightened."

The Only Thing to Fear Is Fear Itself

Then she gave me a parable. "Imagine a woman fleeing from a missile that's about to fall someplace. Will anyone tell her not to flee? No! But if a professional on the topic of ballistics can predict with certainty that the missile will fall precisely where she's running, what should he do? Should he be understanding of her fears and let her run directly to her death, or should he stop her, even by force, and lead her back to the place she's afraid to stand?"

"Of course he should stop her," I replied.

"But she's afraid, poor thing. How can he do that to her? Isn't it cruel?"

"No, Rebbetzin," I said. "It would be cruel to let her continue believing her misplaced fear. She should be stopped. She'll understand later why he was acting in her best interests."

The Rebbetzin smiled for a moment. That was her only smile during our conversation. "She needs to be stopped. She'll understand later," she repeated.

Then her demeanor became angry.

"Listen well. In *Shamayim* there are *neshamos* that need to come to this world, and their serious complaint against you is many times more terrifying than the words of that doctor that haunt you. These *neshamos* are angry with you and are creating a host of bad angels who will persecute you all your life and after your passing, too. The implications are terrible! Your fears don't matter to them at all!"

She paused for a moment and then went on. "You ought to be quaking in fear every moment that you're leaving these *neshamos* in *Shamayim*. Go home and start being scared of the right thing! Don't be afraid of the doctor's unnecessary comment. Be afraid of the terrible *kitrug* (Heavenly allegation) hanging over you. *Daven* to Hashem to annul the decree and give you children. Whatever the price, I Batsheva

Kanievsky, promise you in my name and that of my husband, that your births will go smoothly. Run home and start *davening*," she concluded. "I don't even have time to embrace you. Run home and save your life and your soul."

The Rebbetzin terrified the wits out of me. She frightened me so badly that the doctor and his words flew out of my mind completely. The moment I returned home, I began praying tearfully to be blessed with a child.

Nine months later, my daughter was born with nary a complication, *baruch Hashem*. A year later, we had another son. A year and a half later, we were blessed with another son, and a year after that, with a daughter.

Since then, I've been to the Rebbetzin many times, and each time, she embraced me and showered me with the same words of love she showered on everyone. From time to time, she would ask *mechilah* for the conversation during which she "wasn't nice to me," in her words.

Today I am the mother of five beautiful, healthy children.

My oldest son is seventeen. Our next four children are age eight, seven, five and a half, and four and a half, respectively.

Like everyone else, my husband and I attended the huge *levayah*, which took place this past Sukkos. I left the children with my husband some distance away and did my best to approach the *kever* and bemoan the loss of the esteemed *rebbetzin*, so beloved by so many.

I wanted to tell her, "Thank you for my children. I forgive you with a full heart, even though there's nothing to forgive. You had to stop me from myself, and like the woman in the parable, I really did understand at a later point. Please be a *melitzas yosher* for our five children, for my righteous husband, for me, and for all of *Am Yisrael*."

23

Deceptive Garbage

A sanitation inspector finds a bag of garbage on the sidewalk. He rummages through the bag in search of clues to the owner's identity so he can write out a ticket.

What he finds is a life story that catapults him into an adventure, forcing him to turn from an inspector into a detective.

I've been reading your books for years, and I've noticed that they feature people from all walks of life who have many different occupations, but I'm sure you've never read or written about someone with a job like mine.

My official job description was "sanitation supervisor," but in reality, my job was to rummage through garbage.

When I participated in the tender for the job, conducted by the municipality of the city where I live, I described my previous job experience in the fire department and at a welding workshop and explained to the committee why I thought I was the right man for the job. Suddenly, a member of the committee asked me, "Tell me, do you understand what the job involves?"

"Yes," I replied. "It involves supervising the sanitation in the city."

"And what do you think that means?"

"Uh, reporting if there's anything unsanitary."

"Reporting to whom?"

"To the garbage collectors — if the problem is that they haven't done their job properly."

"And if they have?"

"Well, I guess that should be reported as well."

"But what if they've done their job but the street is still dirty?" he asked.

"That's impossible. If they did their job properly, the street would be clean, wouldn't it?"

"Not at all," replied the fellow, whom I later learned was the director of the sanitation department. "Sometimes, someone decides to put a garbage bag on the sidewalk twelve hours before the next garbage pickup. Sometimes people decide to empty the contents of their apartments, including furniture and other large articles, onto the sidewalk. Sometimes people trim their hedges and leave piles of branches scattered across the pavement. Obviously, the garbage men can't be blamed for such situations."

"So what can you do in such a case?" I asked.

"You can give a citation to the people responsible."

"Oh," I said. "I see. I didn't think of that."

"And what do you understand now?" he asked.

"That if I'm hired for this job, I'll also have to issue citations for such infractions. What's not to understand?"

"But how will you know whom to fine? There might be sixteen families living in one building. How will you know which of them is responsible?"

"I'll ask," I replied.

Deceptive Garbage

"Wonderful," said the director, and I thought we were finally getting somewhere.

I was wrong.

"Let's say I put out a pile of garbage on the sidewalk and you come along and ask me who did it, what do you think I'll reply?"

"You're right," I admitted. "Asking wouldn't work. So what do you do?"

"The answer is precisely the reason I'm talking to you in riddles," he said. "I wanted to inform you that your job will include rummaging through garbage bags to try and find a paper or envelope that will tell you the identity of the person you need to ticket. Now do you understand the nature of the job you're applying for?"

I understood. There was no better way to make me back out of the job.

"Are you trying to persuade me not to take the job?" I asked.

"Not at all," replied a different member of the committee. "He just wants to make sure you're aware of what the job entails. There's no point in hiring you if it's only a matter of time until you discover that you don't want to do it."

I thought for a moment and said, "It's not a problem. I need a job, and I'll take whatever's available."

◄ ◄ ◄

To my surprise, I was hired.

Why was I so surprised? Because if there had been a test, I surely would have failed it. But somehow, out of twelve contenders for the job, I won. Perhaps the others backed out once they heard what was involved; I don't know.

I must note that the director made the job sound worse

than it is. In all honesty, it involves a lot more than checking garbage cans.

Garbage clearance is a fascinating topic, one that most people know almost nothing about. It's understandable, really; it *is* an unpleasant topic. But let the sanitation workers strike for a few days, and suddenly everyone understands just how crucial the job is.

A sanitation inspector must make sure that the sanitation workers did their job properly, taking the garbage cans out of their enclosures. He must ensure that residents don't turn the enclosures into storage areas, and also that they place their garbage bags inside the cans.

With time, you get to know the residents. To parody the well-known adage: "Show me your garbage and I'll tell you who you are."

Most people are okay, I must say, but the minority can ruin it for the majority.

Some people have zero consideration for their neighbors. They place their garbage near the cans, rather than inside them, and the cats come and have a field day. Some people go so far as to simply toss the garbage out the window, hoping it will somehow land in the garbage dumpster.

It wasn't my job to educate people; my job was to make sure the street stayed clean.

If I saw an offending bag of garbage, I had to check the contents in order to find out the identity of the culprit and ticket him so that hopefully, he'd be more careful in the future.

You wouldn't believe how much information you can garner about a person by checking his garbage. It's usually very simple to figure out whom the bag belongs to: a wedding invitation or any torn envelope yields that information. But

Deceptive Garbage

it goes beyond that; the sky's the limit on what you can find out.

For one thing, you might learn a person's bank balance. (The balances in the bank statements I saw were not that great. That's understandable, though, considering most wealthy people live in private homes as opposed to crowded buildings, which is where most offending garbage bags are found.) In a few seconds of rummaging through a garbage bag, you find notes from teachers about the children, copies of contracts, photocopies of personal documents, sensitive medical information and more.

I hope you're not getting the impression that I used my job as an excuse to snoop into people's lives, because the truth is that I never did this unless I had to find out who was responsible for being irresponsible with his garbage. The truth is that more often than not, I knew whom a certain bag belonged to just on sight, but the law required that I have evidence in order to write a ticket, so I had to find at least one document with proof.

One day, I was checking through a bag when I suddenly spotted a piece of paper filled with close writing.

There was no name on that paper, so I looked for an envelope or something with a name, but suddenly one line on the piece of paper seemed to jump out at me. It said, in Hebrew, "*Me'ayin yavo ezri?* — From whence will come my salvation?"

I took another look. The writing was clearly that of a child or an adolescent. It bespoke terrible distress.

Two voices battled inside me. One said, "Drop it. It's none of your business." The other said, "You can't ignore this."

I took the letter.

Later, in the privacy of my car, I sat down to read it.

It wasn't addressed to anyone.

It had been written by a young boy in *yeshivah ketanah*. Apparently, he had written it as a way of expressing his feelings.

He wrote that he had no friends and that he couldn't confide in his parents (he didn't write why). The words were laden with despair. He described the torture his peers put him through and the agony of having no one to talk to. It was clear that he was lonely, humiliated and hurt to the core of his soul.

He wrote that on the fast of *Asarah BeTeves*, he'd completed all of *sefer Tehillim*, *davening* to Hashem for his situation to improve. He described his emotional pain so vividly that I felt my own heart begin to ache.

The next paragraph made it clear that this boy was in a terrible emotional state and that he needed help urgently.

I didn't know the boy's name, but I was familiar with his family. From one side, I had no problem calling his parents, but at the same time, I had a huge problem calling his parents. What should I tell them? That I had invaded their privacy?

I'd never experienced such a dilemma before. On the one hand, here was a youth experiencing emotional difficulty; on the other, I couldn't do a thing about it — except continuing to keep track of their garbage.

A week later, there was another letter. This time, the boy's distress was even more acute. He mentioned the names of two *bachurim* who were causing him to "hate my life." Those were his words. He described the terrible things they did to make his life miserable. When I read that description, I broke down in tears. Was it any wonder the boy was in a terrible emotional state? He was literally shunned by his classmates.

Deceptive Garbage

Apparently, the only time they spoke with him was in order to taunt him.

His emotional state was contagious. I felt a terrible heaviness spread through my limbs. It bothered me to no end that I was aware of this young boy's suffering yet was doing nothing to help him.

I considered many possibilities: Should I send the letter to the boy's parents? No, I had no right to do that. Should I figure out which yeshivah he attended and speak with one of its heads? Even worse. Should I contact the boy directly? That would be very strange on my part, and illegal to boot.

I was terrified. I was ready to do anything, but my hands were tied.

✉   ✉   ✉

I decided to discuss the matter with my wife.

I told her the story and showed her the letters. She agreed that it would be wrong to use them, but that I couldn't sit idly by and let the situation continue without doing something.

I told her I knew that I risked losing my job if I helped the boy. I was prepared to do that; but I had no way of helping him without hurting him.

If I contacted him, he was liable to be very upset, and rightfully so. I had unforgivably invaded his privacy by reading his letters.

"How about contacting his parents?" my wife suggested.

"How would you react if a stranger called you and told you he'd read a letter written by your son?"

My wife considered for a moment and said, "I'm not sure. I think I might be appreciative — especially now that we're having this experience. But I have an idea. *You* won't call them; I'll call. When a woman calls, it's somehow less threatening."

"You have a point," I agreed. "What will you say, that you're a sanitation inspector?"

"No," she replied, her tone of voice so put out that I couldn't help but feel insulted. "I'll introduce myself as the mother of one of the students in the class. I'll say that my son has been telling me that her son seems very unhappy."

"Great idea," I enthused. "Let's do it."

We got the phone number. My wife read the letters a few more times to help her get into the role.

Then she dialed the number.

After a moment that seemed like an eternity, a woman answered. "Hello," my wife said. "Is this Mrs. Riklin (not their real name)?"

"Speaking."

"Look, I'm the mother of a student in the same yeshivah your son attends. For the past few weeks, my son has been telling me that your son is suffering socially and that he thinks he might be depressed. I thought I should tell you in case you don't know."

"I think you've made a mistake," the woman replied.

"Isn't this the Riklin family?"

"It is."

My wife began to lose her nerve, but she forged on. "Maybe you haven't noticed, but my son comes home every day and says your son looks so miserable, even depressed."

"My son is not depressed," the woman said resolutely. "In fact, he passed away more than five years ago after a bout with cancer."

My wife was in shock. We hadn't expected such a thing. "I'm sorry," she mumbled. "I must have made a mistake."

We couldn't bear to look each other in the eye. I have never been so ashamed of something I'd done.

Deceptive Garbage

"Those letters must have been written more than five years ago," my wife said, weeping profusely. "Poor *bachur*, how he must have suffered before his death. I also pity the boys who tortured him; they probably never had a chance to ask for forgiveness."

We sat there in silence, and my wife read the letters once again. Suddenly she said, "Wait a minute, there's a date here." She pointed to a date on the top of the page. "This letter was written last week," she said, pointing to the date on the second letter, "and this one," she said, examining the first one, "was written the week before that. Something doesn't add up. How can he be writing letters if he passed away?"

This enigma was too incredible to be real. We sat there, two simple people contending with a tremendously perplexing riddle.

We struggled to come up with an explanation.

"Maybe we have the wrong family?" my wife suggested.

"No," I said. "I checked in so many ways. It's definitely that family's garbage bag."

"Maybe she just made up a story to get rid of you," I said, regretting my words as soon as they were out of my mouth.

Despite our curiosity, my wife and I decided to stop our involvement in the matter. I had already crossed many boundaries for the boy in distress. The boy was no longer alive. There was no justification in continuing to snoop through the family's trash.

Two weeks went by. Every time I passed the building, I felt my heart begin to pound. The enigma was giving me no rest.

A few weeks later, on a Friday, I saw several garbage bags

next to the building's dumpster rather than inside it.

I took one bag, opened it, and began looking for envelopes or some sort of proof.

I came across a letter by the same boy.

My heart began to pound. I picked up the letter and began reading it, and just then, I heard a hesitant voice behind me say, "Excuse me, sir. It's... it's not right, what you're doing. That's private stuff."

I saw a boy who seemed about fifteen years old.

"I'm a sanitation inspector," I said, "and I have to know whom this bag belongs to."

"That's not true," the boy said. "You started reading my letter, and..."

"Is this your letter?" I practically shouted.

"Shhh," he said. "It's private. It's really not right that you're reading stuff you find in the garbage. I'm going to lodge a complaint against you."

"You're alive, then?" I shouted.

He grew alarmed and took a step back. "What do you want from me?" he asked. "Are you really a sanitation inspector? I don't think so!"

I regained some semblance of control. "Here's my card," I said, withdrawing my worker's ID card. "I know my behavior seems strange, but you must hear my story."

He still looked hesitant and suspicious, but he said, "Go ahead."

"Look, as I said, I'm a sanitation supervisor, My job is to identify the owners of garbage bags not placed inside the garbage and ticket them. A few weeks ago, I came across your letters. They affected me deeply but I didn't know how to help you. My wife and I thought of a way to help you, but it didn't work because..."

Deceptive Garbage

"So you read the previous letters, too?"

"Yes," I said. "I'm so sorry. It's from *Shamayim*. I mean, the letters were from the garbage, but it's all from *Shamayim*."

The boy couldn't help but chuckle, and after a moment, I joined in.

I explained quickly that in addition to being a sanitation inspector, I was married and the father of children, and that when I came across such letters — I felt that I must do something to try and help.

"I understand that," he said. After a moment's pause, he added cynically, "Not that I actually received any help."

"You wouldn't believe what we did," I told him. "My wife called your mother pretending to be the mother of one of your friends and she told her that you're suffering greatly."

"Really?" the boy asked tensely.

"Yes, she was hoping your mother would find a way to help you."

"And how did my mother react?"

"I don't know how to say this…"

"Tell me."

"I can't."

"Go on, tell me."

"Do you have a brother who died of cancer?"

"No."

"But that's what she said."

"She said I had a brother who died of cancer?" He sounded horrified.

"My wife told her that her son seemed very unhappy, and she said that… her son had died five years ago… of cancer."

The moment I uttered those words, I was sure that I had made a terrible mistake. Hearing that was all the poor boy needed.

But rather than be upset he began to laugh and laugh. I didn't understand what was going on.

"Your wife must have spoken to my grandmother. She's not well and her memory is failing her. My uncle, her son, passed away five years ago. She didn't understand that you were talking about me, which I think is a good thing."

📣   📣   📣

The enigma was solved. I breathed a sigh of relief. The boy who wrote the letters was standing opposite me and he seemed perfectly fine; he was not a ghost, nor did his mother act as if he were dead. But the letter in my hand was just one of three witnesses that he still needed help desperately.

"Listen to me," I said. "I haven't come this far in vain. You are a fifteen-year-old *bachur* dealing with a very difficult and painful situation. I know you didn't want to tell anyone what you're going through, but *Hakadosh Baruch Hu* gave me this job. I know this is neither the time nor place, but take my phone number, and I will find someone to help you."

He took my card, appearing very deeply moved.

I smiled at him and said, "I'm warning you; you'd better call. Otherwise I'll call your house and this time, I won't talk to your grandmother. Is that clear?"

He smiled and said, "Don't do a thing until I call you. Don't tell anyone my name."

I gave him my word.

I contacted Social Services in our city and spoke to someone who works with teens. I told him the story and he instructed me what to tell the boy in order to persuade him to agree to get counseling.

The next day, the boy called. I put him in touch with my contact at Social Services and they met.

After that, I bowed out of the picture and received no further updates for a while. Months later, the boy called me. He told me that he had received devoted care that had helped him overcome his social problems. He'd learned to be more assertive with the boys who had hurt him so badly and slowly regained footing among his peers.

Two days later, I spoke to my contact at Social Services, who told me, "You should know that you saved this boy's life."

These words were like a balm to my soul. They made me realize that there was a reason that I had been given this job.

A few years passed. I no longer work as a sanitation inspector. I opened an independent business and thank God, I'm doing well. But I'll never forget my job as a sanitation inspector — not because of the smell, but because I know the reason God sent me to serve in that capacity.

24

The Grand Scheme

On yet another trip to the Kosel, our Yerushalmi's wife risks serious trouble with the "managers of the Kosel" due to a job description she assumes of her own volition.

Our friend is forced to tell a somewhat uncomfortable personal story about his son Shaya'leh. You see, Shaya'leh is on pills.

Actually, the news is not really all that earth-shattering. After all, all of Meah Shearim already knows...

It's me again, the Yerushalmi Yid, and I have another story to tell you.

Approximately two weeks ago, we took a taxi to the Kosel, because we no longer have the strength to walk there from Meah Shearim the way we used to.

At the Kosel, I parted from my wife, who made her way to the women's section, while I went to *daven Minchah* and recite some *Tehillim* in the men's section.

When I was done, I waited for my wife to finish her affairs in the women's section. When I say "affairs," I mean not only

The Grand Scheme

davening and reciting *Tehillim*, but also — as I have reported on in my previous letters to — she opens a mobile "welfare" office for women in distress who come to the Kosel as a last resort. She listens to their complaints and *tzaros* and tries to console them and help if possible.

You must surely be wondering how the women know to approach my wife. There are two explanations for this.

First, my wife is one of the oldest Kosel-goers around. She's been going regularly ever since it was liberated during the Six Day War. All it takes is one woman to recognize her, and before you know it, everyone is clamoring to get close to her and ask her advice. Based on rumors I've heard, she also dispenses blessings.

The same rumors tell me that women at the Kosel call my wife "*rabbanit*," even though there is no justification for this whatsoever. After all, a *rabbanit* is the wife of a *rav*, which I am not.

Of course, I don't tell my wife about these rumors lest she suspect (with good reason) that I listen to gossip about her or spy on her.

The second reason is that even if my wife is not recognized by anyone at the Kosel, she goes out of her way to initiate contact with women who have problems. She tells them that she knows what they're going through, and human nature is such that when someone begins describing the difficulty of what you're going through, you open up to her. If you happen to be wondering how my wife knows about women's *tzaros* before they tell her, allow me to remind you of my wife's controversial custom of peeking at the notes women place in the cracks of the Kosel. Actually, "peeking" is the wrong word; she reads them with great interest from beginning to end.

I usually have to wait quite awhile until my wife completes her affairs, because I make do with *tefillah* and *Tehillim* while she adds her welfare services, so we can never be ready at the same time. I'm always ready to leave before her. But this time she seemed to be even later than usual.

In the end, when she finally arrived at our meeting place near the steps, I noticed that she wasn't alone. She was accompanied by another woman, which was most unusual. They drew closer, and my wife apologized for her lateness, explaining that the welfare department at the Kosel had been unusually busy. She added that she had asked the woman at her side to come with her so that I would tell her a certain story.

I had waited more than the usual amount of time as it was, and the thought of telling a story right then was not appealing at all. Still, I said not a word to my wife, sensing that she might be hurt, oblivious as she was to the fact that I'd been waiting in the sun for far too long and would like nothing better than to go home already.

Instead, I asked, "Which story did you want me to tell?"

"When you know what her problem is, you'll know what story to tell. I brought you the note she wrote so you can see her problem."

I looked at the note and saw immediately that it wasn't addressed to me. Every time I open a letter, I check to see if the greeting includes my name in order to avoid accidentally reading something not intended for my eyes. In this letter, the greeting read: "To God in Heaven." Neither the name nor the address were mine, so I knew that the letter was intended for Someone else.

"Uh, I think this letter belongs between the cracks in the Kosel," I said gently to my wife, but the woman at her side

The Grand Scheme

hurried to placate me. "Yes, I placed it between the stones at the Kosel, but your wife, who is in charge of the notes at the Kosel, just happened to be there."

I looked around to make sure no one had overheard her, because taking notes out of the cracks is one thing, but declaring yourself "in charge" of the notes is quite another. I was afraid someone from the Kosel management might hear about my wife's self-appointment, carried out without the involvement of anyone else. They might immediately cancel the appointment or even worse, take legal action against my wife.

I decided to take matters into my own hands and read the note without asking for any further explanations.

What was written in the note?

Dear God in Heaven, please make my son (here the child's full name and that of his mother appeared) *agree to take the pills that help him study Torah.*

"She's probably referring to the same pills that our son took, no?"

My wife glared at me and said, "Lower your voice! Someone might hear you!"

"All of Meah Shearim knows that our son is on pills," I said. "Why should you care if this woman knows, too?"

My wife gave me that look that means I've overstepped my bounds and will be made to pay for it. Before I had a chance to regret my question, the woman at her side added fuel to the fire and said eagerly, "You mean your son is on pills, too?"

"Not quite," my wife replied, sounding annoyed at the woman she was trying to help. "None of our children takes pills, but one of our sons *told* everyone that he takes pills."

"I know lots of people who take pills but don't tell anyone," the woman said dubiously, "but I've never heard of anyone who doesn't take pills and tells people that he does. It sounds to me as though just for this behavior he ought to be on medication."

This woman was obviously sharp-tongued and very brave. I didn't say a word, though, because I understood that it would not be proper for me to support her when my wife was under attack, or at least she felt that way. So I held my tongue.

"So, as the woman in charge of the notes at the Kosel, do you intend to tell me what I should do about my son?" the woman asked.

She wasn't merely impudent, this woman, she was behaving as though my wife worked for her even though she hadn't paid her a red cent. I wanted to open my mouth and retort but then I realized that it was possible my wife had presented herself as the supervisor of the notes at the Kosel — and if I denied that, I'd be working against her…

So before matters became more complicated, I said to her: "I'll tell you the whole story and you can draw your own conclusions as to whether or not our son is on medication."

And then I told her about my son Yeshayahu, whom we call Shaya'leh.

Shaya'leh is a *melamed* at a Talmud Torah. (Don't confuse him with his brother, the one who was an underachiever as a boy but then married a girl from Haifa, the daughter of the Judaica merchant, and then became not only a *mensch* but the manager of a Talmud Torah.) Shaya'leh was always

The Grand Scheme

a wonderful son, and after studying in *kollel* for a while, he began teaching in a Talmud Torah.

A few years ago, there were rumors that Shaya'leh was on pills.

In Meah Shearim, it doesn't take more than two minutes from the time that one person learns a certain tidbit of information until the entire neighborhood knows.

I thought to myself: *Oy vey, Shaya'leh's on pills, but how does the whole community know?*

But I didn't say a word to Shaya'leh, and I warned my wife not to say anything either.

This might sound strange, but my approach has always been that if something was not told to me explicitly, apparently the person involved didn't want me to know, and if that was the case, my questioning him would only cause him discomfort or distress.

In rare cases when I thought I might be able to help but the subject was ashamed to ask, I came up with a way to check whether this was indeed so. But in this case, if Shaya'leh was taking pills, apparently he had dealt with the situation on his own.

Of course, it pained me that my son needed medication, but I worked to overcome that pain because my son didn't have to suffer as a result of my nerves.

🕮 🕮 🕮

One day, Shaya'leh approached me and said, "You probably heard that I'm on pills."

I was alarmed by his direct manner and scrambled to come up with an appropriate response. "Yes, I've heard something to that effect," I replied. "Although I was concerned, I trusted that you would tell me if you felt it was necessary."

"I want to tell you and Ima how the rumor came about."

That year, Shaya'leh had a student who was impossible to teach. In the course of a single lesson, he would drag kids' backpacks around, shoot spitballs at the *melamed* and at the children, yell, hit, and walk freely around the room.

In previous years, the child had spent most of his time outside the classroom and a considerable amount of time suspended from the Talmud Torah.

The truth is that in my time, too, we had such children. The obvious question is, if rambunctious children always existed, how come the rambunctious children of previous generations didn't dare behave the way today's kids do. I say it's because of the *potches* we used to get, and I ask you to please refer to the letter in which I tell the story about Leibele's will to understand what type of *chinuch* I'm referring to.

Ordinary rambunctious kids sat and learned — or at least sat.

Only the truly wild would get into mischief from time to time, although they were never openly naughty, and when they were caught, they paid the price.

But nowadays it's forbidden to *potch*, and the children allow themselves to do as they please, which is why they came up with these pills. I think it's safe to say that a once-a-month *potch* achieved the same effect as a ten-milligram dose of Ritalin or Concerta.

᠅ ᠅ ᠅

When Shaya'leh saw that this boy couldn't sit still, he contacted his father and asked him why he wasn't doing something about the situation.

The father told my son that the doctor had prescribed medication but that his son refused to take it. His parents assured

The Grand Scheme

him that no one would know he was taking the pills, but he still refused. Apparently, he was ashamed even of himself.

My son asked if they had tried anything else, and the father told him that they had tried all sorts of holistic remedies but that while they had created a serious dent in his wallet, they hadn't helped at all.

And then Shaya'leh said to the father, "Bring me a box of your son's medication, please."

"What for?" the father asked, taken aback. Shaya'leh said simply, "You'll see."

The following day, the father met Shaya'leh at *Shacharis* and slipped him a box of pills. Shaya'leh made sure the father hadn't said a word to his son about the matter.

Later, Shaya'leh was in middle of teaching when his cell phone rang.

Normally, Shaya'leh never speaks on the phone in middle of class, but in this case he deviated from his custom.

This is how the conversation went:

"Hello? Yes, of course. Is it something urgent?"

"Oh, right. It's a good thing you reminded me. I really did forget to take my pill this morning. Thanks for reminding me. I'll take it right now. Have a good day."

He hung up the phone and told his students, "It's a good thing my wife called to remind me that I forgot to take my pill this morning. I was already feeling that it was hard for me to teach and I couldn't understand why." He paused for a moment and then said, "Who wants to bring me my pills?"

Of course, the whole class volunteered. Shaya'leh scanned the classroom and called on the child who needed the medication but was ashamed to take it. "On the counter in the teachers' room is a black bag with a box of pills inside. Take the box out of the bag and bring it to me, please."

The boy ran off, found the bag, and withdrew a familiar box that looked just like the one he had at home.

He brought it to the *melamed*, who said, "Would you mind bringing me a cup of water, too?"

The child brought a cup of water and Shaya'leh said to the whole class, "These pills are called Concerta. They're good for people who have a hard time concentrating. You can't imagine how many *masechtos* you can finish when you take these pills. I take one every day so that I can teach you properly, but today I forgot."

And my son took a pill and swallowed it, just like that.

Guess what happened next? A different child piped up and said, "I take such pills, too."

"I take a different pill, called Ritalin," another one spoke up. "It's also to help me concentrate."

The following day, the recalcitrant child took his medication without a fuss. He was the quietest boy in the class that day! The same scenario repeated itself the following day and every day thereafter. Before long, this child, whom the school administration had been threatening to expel from the Talmud Torah, became one of the top boys in the class.

One of the children in the class told his father that Shaya'leh took pills. Shocked, the father asked around to check whether this was true. The other children confirmed that the *melamed* himself had told them that he was on pills, and that they had even seen him take one during class. That's how the rumor spread throughout Meah Shearim, eventually reaching my ears.

I kissed Shaya'leh on the forehead and said, "My son, I am so impressed at the lengths to which you went in order to

The Grand Scheme

help your student. I promise you no harm will come of it."

A few months later, everyone knew the truth about why Shaya'leh had done what he'd done, but the identity of the boy he had helped remained a secret. The father who had made the whole fuss about Shaya'leh's being on medication became his ardent admirer.

"That's the story in short," I said to the woman. "I suggest that you ask your son's *melamed* to do the same thing as Shaya'leh. Don't worry, there's no harm in taking one of the pills. He doesn't have to take it in front of the whole class; he can stage the incident so that it takes place only in front of your son, in the teachers' room. He should be sure to make it seem as though it's just a coincidence that your son is there when he takes it. I hope my Shaya'leh's idea will help your son, too."

We said goodbye and hurried to flag down a cab.

My wife was tense and curious whether the woman would take our advice and whether the child's *melamed* would agree to do what Shaya'leh had done for his student.

My wife had another concern: What if the woman hadn't fully understood and she thought our Shaya'leh really was on medication?

In the end, we learned that the woman had misunderstood us, but in a different way. A few days after our meeting at the Kosel, she called our home and filled us in on what had happened.

Mr. Walder, if you happen to be standing, I suggest you sit down, because this might induce a headache or heartache: The first thing the woman did upon arriving home was to tell her son the whole story.

Can you believe the brilliance of this woman? She told him about Shaya'leh's scheme, completely ruining the one chance she had at getting him to take his medication!

So what happened?

Here's the real surprise: Apparently, her son is even less bright than she is. When he heard the story, he got so excited that from that day on, he began taking his medication without a fuss. She was barely able to restrain him from taking the pills to school.

Go understand people.

I used to think that foolishness was a disease, but in this case, it was the medication. Pun intended.

Glossary

The following glossary provides a partial explanation of some of the Hebrew, Yiddish (Y.), and Aramaic (A.) words and phrases used in this book. The spellings and explanations reflect the way the specific word is used herein. Often, there are alternate spellings and meanings for the words.

A"H: a Hebrew acronym for "May s/he rest in peace."
AHAVAS HATORAH: love of Torah.
AL KIDDUSH HASHEM: for sanctification of the Divine Name; martyrdom.
ALIYAH: lit., "ascent"; immigration to Israel.
AM YISRAEL: the Nation of Israel.
ASARAH BETEVES: 10th of Teves, a fast day.
AVREICH: a married, young Torah scholar.
AYIN HARA: the evil eye.
BA'AL TESHUVAH: a formerly non-observant Jew who has returned to Jewish tradition and practice.
BACHUR: a young man; a yeshivah student.
BAR MITZVAH: a boy who has reached the age of thirteen years, when he is considered to have attained full religious responsibility; the ceremony marking a Jewish boy's thirteenth birthday.
BARUCH HASHEM: "Thank God!"
BAS: daughter of.
BASHERT: (Y.) pre-destined.
BEIN HAZEMANIM: a yeshiva vacation period.

BEIS DIN: a rabbinical court of law.
BEN TORAH: a person devoted to a Torah way of life.
BERACHAH: a blessing.
BIRKAS HAGOMEL: the blessing recited after surviving a dangerous experience; the blessing recited before the opened Torah scroll by one who has been rescued or has escaped from danger.
BRIS: lit., "covenant"; ritual circumcision.
CHAREIDI: an ultra-Orthodox Jew.
CHAS V'SHALOM: "God forbid!"
CHASAN: a bridegroom.
CHAZAL: an acronym for "our Sages, of blessed memory."
CHEDER: lit., "room"; (Y., colloq.) a Jewish primary school for boys.
CHESED: kindness.
CHIDDUSHEI TORAH: Torah novellae.
CHILLUL HASHEM: desecration of God's Name.
CHINUCH: [Jewish] education.
CHOLENT: a stew, usually containing meat, potatoes and beans, which is kept hot overnight and served on Shabbos day.
CHOLIM: the sick.
CHUPPAH: a wedding canopy; a wedding.
DA'AS TORAH: the accepted, Torah-based opinions of recognized rabbinic authorities.
DATI: religious.
DAVEN: (Y.) pray.
DAYAN: a judge in a Jewish court.
DERECH: [proper] path.
DIN TORAH: lit., "Torah law"; a dispute judged by a rabbinical court in accordance with Halachah.
DIVREI TORAH: words of Torah.
DVAR TORAH: a Torah discourse.
EISHES CHAYIL: a woman of valor.
EREV TEFILLAH: a gathering for an evening of prayer.
FARHER: (Y.) oral examination or review.
GA'AVAH: pride.
GALUS: exile.

Glossary

GEDOLIM: lit., "greats"; Torah authorities.

GEMARA: commentary and discussion of the Mishnah (together they comprise the Talmud).

GUTTE NESHAMAH: (Y.) a good soul.

HACHNASAS KALLAH: dowering a bride; a bridal fund.

HAKADOSH BARUCH HU: lit., "the Holy One, Blessed be He"; God.

HALACHAH: Jewish law.

HASHEM: God.

HASHKAFAH: [Torah] outlook.

HAVDALAH: lit., "separation"; the ceremony marking the conclusion of Sabbaths and Festivals, separating the holy day from the other days of the week.

HESPED: a eulogy.

HETER: leniency.

HISHTADLUS: the obligation to provide human effort to alleviate a situation, with the realization that the result of these efforts is ultimately in God's hands.

KABBALAH: an acceptance; accepting upon oneself a resolution.

KADDISH: a prayer sanctifying God's Name; the mourner's prayer.

KALLAH: a bride.

KAPPARAS AVONOS: an atonement for sin.

KEHILLAH: a Jewish community or congregation.

KEVER: a grave.

KIBBUTZ: a small, usually rural, Israeli collective.

KIRUV: bringing non or less observant Jews closer to Torah observance.

KISEI HAKAVOD: the Heavenly Throne.

KOLLEL: a center for advanced Torah study for adult students, mostly married men.

LAMDAN: Torah scholar possessing an in-depth knowledge of the Talmud.

LASHON HARA: evil speech.

LESHEM SHAMAYIM: for the sake of Heaven.

LEVAYAH: a funeral.

LISHMAH: "for its own sake"; usually refers to learning Torah.

MA'ARIV: the evening prayer service.

MAROR: bitter herbs, eaten on Passover.

MASECHTOS: tractates.

MASHGIACH: religious supervisor/spiritual guide in a yeshivah.

MAZAL: luck.

MECHANECHES: female educator.

MECHILAH: forgiveness.

MECHITZAH: the partition which separates the men's and women's sections in a synagogue.

MECHUTANIM: the parents of one's son- or daughter-in-law.

MEKUBAL: a Kabbalist.

MELAMED: a Torah teacher of school-age children.

MELITZAS YOSHER: an advocate (female).

MENAHEL: a prinicpal.

MENSCH: (Y.) lit., "a man"; an upstanding human being.

MIDDOS: character traits.

MIN HASHAMAYIM: lit., "from Heaven."

MINCHAH: the afternoon prayer service.

MINYAN: a quorum of ten men required for public prayer service.

MUSSAR: ethical teachings; Torah ethics and values aimed at character improvement.

NACHAS: pride; pleasure; satisfaction.

NEBACH: (Y.) "poor thing!"

NESHAMAH: soul.

NISAYON: a trial or test.

NUSACH: order or specific wording of prayers, of which there are slightly variant versions.

OY: (Y.) "Oh!"

OY VEY: (Y.) "Oh my!"

PARASHAH: [Torah] portion.

PARNASAH: livelihood.

PASUK: a Scriptural verse.

PIDYON HABEN: redemption of the firstborn.

PIKUACH NEFESH: saving a human life.

POTCH: (Y.) a smack.

Glossary

RA"M: a Talmud lecturer in a yeshivah.
RABBANIM: rabbis.
RABBANIT: the wife of a rabbi.
RAV: a rabbi; a teacher.
REBBETZIN: (Y.) the wife of a rabbi.
REFUAH SHELEIMAH: a speedy recovery.
ROSH YESHIVAH: the head of a yeshivah.
SEFER: a book; a holy book.
SEGULAH: a supra-logical action which has practical effects.
SERUV: a document issued by a religious court against someone who refuses to comply with the court.
SEUDAH SHLISHIS: the third meal on Shabbos.
SEUDAS HODA'AH: a festive meal held to give thanks to God for being saved from a life-and-death situation.
SHACHARIS: the morning prayer service.
SHADCHAN: a matchmaker.
SHALOM ZACHAR: the celebration in Ashkenazic homes on the first Friday night after the birth of a boy.
SHAMAYIM: Heaven.
SHEKEL: Israeli currency.
SHIDDUCH: a marital match.
SHIUR KLALI: a lecture on a general topic, which is used to explain numerous passages, rather than a lecture explaining the meaning or logic of a specific passage.
SHIVAH: joy; a joyous occasion.
SHLITA: a Hebrew acronym for "May he live long."
SHLOSHIM: lit., "thirty"; the thirty-day mourning period after the death of a close relative.
SHVER: (Y.) father-in-law.
SIMCHAH: happiness; a joyous occasion.
SUGYA: (Y.) a specific topic of Talmudic discussion.
TALMID CHACHAM: a Torah scholar.
TEFILLAH: prayer.
TEFILLIN: phylacteries.
TEHILLIM: the Book of Psalms.

TESHUVAH: repentance.
TREIF: non-kosher.
TZADDIK: a pious, righteous man.
TZADEKES: (Y.) a righteous, pious woman.
TZAROS: troubles; misfortune.
TZEDAKAH: charity.
TZIBBUR: congregation.
TZITZIS: knotted fringes attached to four-cornered garments worn by Jewish males to remind them of God and His commandments.
TZNIUS: modesty.
YAHRTZEIT: (Y.) the anniversary of a death.
YARMULKE: (Y.) a skullcap.
YEKKE: a Jew of Germanic descent.
YESHIVAH BACHUR: a yeshivah student.
YESHIVAH GEDOLAH: a Torah academy for post-high-school-age boys.
YESHIVAH KETANAH: a Torah academy for teenage boys.
YESHUAH: a salvation.
YETZER HARA: the evil inclination.
YETZER TOV: the good inclination.
YICHUS; lineage.
YID: (Y.) a Jew.
YIDDISHKEIT: (Y.) Judaism.
YIZKOR: memorial service for the deceased.
YIRAS SHAMAYIM: fear of Heaven.
Z"L: a Hebrew acronym for "May his memory be for a blessing."
ZEMIROS: songs.